*Apr 06*

*Fasta Jeremiah*
*Shalom in o...*
*Rabbi Leo ...*
*+*
*Messianic Rabbi Barney Kasdan*

# GOD'S APPOINTED TIMES

A Practical Guide For Understanding
and Celebrating The Biblical Holy Days

## Barney Kasdan

Lederer Books
a division of
**Messianic Jewish Publishers**
Baltimore

Printed in the United States of America

09  08  07  06  05  04            14  13  12  11  10  9
ISBN  1-880226-54-5


Library of Congress Catalog Control Number: 96216368


Lederer Books
a division of
MESSIANIC JEWISH PUBISHERS
6204 Park Heights Ave.
Baltimore, Maryland  21215
(410) 358-6471

Distributed by
Messianic Jewish Resources International
Order line: (800) 410-7367
E-mail: lederer@messianicjewish.net
Website: www.messianicjewish.net

# Table of Contents

A Word from the Author                                               v

Chapter 1:   Shabbat—The Sabbath                                      1

Chapter 2:   Pesach—The Passover                                     25

Chapter 3:   Sfirat HaOmer—The Early First Fruits                   39

Chapter 4:   Shavuot—The Latter First Fruits                        51

Chapter 5:   Rosh HaShanah—The New Year                             63

Chapter 6:   Yom Kippur—The Day of Atonement                        77

Chapter 7:   Sukkot—The Feast of Tabernacles                        91

Chapter 8:   Hanukkah—The Feast of Dedication                      107

Chapter 9:   Purim—The Feast of Lots                               121

Conclusion:  The Joy of the Holidays                               133

Bibliography                                                       134

# Acknowledgments

I would like to thank a number of people who were instrumental in the completion of this book. Kathy McGrath was a tremendous help with her expertise in formating and with many of the graphics.

Thomas Solomon added much to this work with his ideas and creative graphics. Much of the music, which I know will be a blessing to many people, was compiled by Dr. Sebastian Winston with the computer help of Chris Vitas.

A special thanks goes to all the wonderful members of Kehilat Ariel Messianic Congregation of San Diego, California for their encouragement. In a real sense, this congregation served as a living laboratory to test how all the biblical holy days can be applied for believers in Yeshua as Messiah.

I so appreciate Barry Rubin and Lederer Messianic Publications for support and direction in the publication of this book.

My wife, Liz Kasdan, deserves special recognition for not only compiling the wonderful recipes, but for being a true helpmate in every aspect of our life together.

Finally, all glory goes to my redeemer, Messiah Yeshua, whom I understand even better through the appointed times of my heavenly father. Blessed be he!

# A Word from the Author about God's Appointed Times

## A SEARCH FOR JEWISH ROOTS

Something unusual is stirring among believers in Yeshua (Jesus) in our day. You must have noticed since you are interested in a book like this.

Throughout Church history there has been a chasm of misunderstanding between the Church (the body of Messiah) and the Jewish people. Both Christians and Jews have falsely concluded that there is little real or practical connection between Christianity and Jewish life. However, these views are based on either ignorance or false presuppositions.

As one objectively studies the New Testament, one finds there is no escaping the inherent Jewishness of faith in Yeshua, the Messiah. Jesus himself was a traditional Jew living in the land of Israel. He called other Jews to follow him as *Mashiach* (Messiah), the anointed one from God. His early followers considered themselves to be Jews who had found the promised Messiah; hence, they naturally continued the Jewish expression of their faith.

It is, I believe, a tragedy that the Christian community has not understood, for the most part, the rich heritage on which its faith is built. Many believers, however, rediscovering these connections, are wondering just how they can understand the Jewishness of their faith in a practical way. The biblical holy days are a pragmatic way. These feasts were revealed by God for his own particular reasons, and through them all believers can be blessed, Jews and Gentiles.

## THE PURPOSE OF THE BIBLICAL HOLIDAYS

The Feasts of the Lord, or the biblical holy days, teach us about the nature of God and his plan for mankind. A classic passage in regard to the holy days is found in the New Testament.

> *So don't let anyone pass judgment on you in connection with eating and drinking, or in regard to a Jewish festival or Rosh-Chodesh or Shabbat. These are a shadow of things that are coming, but the body is of the Messiah* (Colossians 2:16–17).

While this passage is often taken to mean "avoid legalism," there is another truth stated. It is true that the "festivals" are not the ultimate goals of faith, yet they do hold tremendous lessons for God's children. The festivals are not antiquated tangents to faith but, on the positive side, they are in fact legitimate shadows or models of God's truth. This is something that should be explored in a positive way, not shunned as legalism.

For example, the Sabbath has much to teach about our weekly lives. Passover is rich in the symbolism of the Messiah's death, burial and resurrection. Rosh HaShanah and Yom Kippur are not obsolete, but continue to declare the reality of Yeshua's return to this earth.

In short, all of the Feasts of the Lord were given to Israel and to "grafted-in" believers to teach, in a practical way, more about God and his plan for the world. When analyzed with the right spirit, there are some exciting new truths waiting to be rediscovered through participation in the Jewish/biblical holy days!

## THE CONTINUITY OF THE BIBLICAL HOLY DAYS

Some believers understand, at least in a theoretical way, that the feasts provide excellent teaching for believers. Yet, because of certain popular theological positions, these believers question the value of continuing the celebrations today. Their contention is that these holy days are no longer relevant because Jesus *fulfilled* all their symbolism in his earthly life and ministry. While there is a fulfillment to the holy days, there is also a continuation of the practical expression of these feasts.

Yeshua himself observed the various feasts during his earthly life. The Gospel writers tell us that his custom was to worship on the Sabbath (Luke 4:16). It was during the Feast of Tabernacles (*Sukkot*) that Yeshua offered "living water" to the Jewish multitude (John 7:37–39). One of his most powerful sermons, in which he proclaimed his Messiahship, took place in the Temple at Hanukkah (John 10:22–30). The earthly life and ministry of Messiah show the continuity of the biblical holy days.

This continuity did not suddenly cease with the apostolic generation that followed. Although there are several statements in the New Testament that cause us to think carefully about a proper balance concerning the holy days, there is clear indication that the early followers of Yeshua continued the practices.

It was at *Shavuot*/Pentecost that the first believers gathered for worship to proclaim the risen Messiah (Acts 2). In his discussion about the spiritual significance of Passover, Paul exhorts the Corinthian believers (a mixed group of Jews and Gentiles) to "celebrate the Seder" (I Corinthians 5:8) with right understanding. There is abundant evidence that the disciples understood and continued to celebrate the wonderful truth of God through the holy days delineated in the Scriptures. This is an example for believers today. Much can be gained by continuing to observe the holy days in the present generation.

## THE FREEDOM OF THE BIBLICAL HOLY DAYS

A final note needs to be made as we consider the celebration of the biblical feasts by believers.

Hopefully you are excited about the positive reasons to understand and incorporate the holy days into your life. Of utmost importance is the emphasis upon our freedom in the

Messiah. These days, as with any other biblical custom, are not meant to lead us into legalistic bondage. Messiah Yeshua is our total sufficiency when it comes to our spiritual standing before God (Galatians 5:1).

Yet, there are some compelling reasons to celebrate the feasts. I hope you will discover, as many believers have, that a balanced celebration of the feasts is a wonderful blessing. The biblical festivals teach much about who God is and his exciting plan for life. It is my prayer that this positive blessing will be yours as you better understand and celebrate God's appointed times!

**BARNEY KASDAN**
**FEBRUARY, 1993**

# Shabbat

The Sabbath

## THE HISTORICAL BACKGROUND

> The Lord said to Moses, "Speak to the Israelites and say to them:
> 'These are my appointed feasts, the appointed feasts of the Lord,
> which you are to proclaim as sacred assemblies. There are six days
> when you may work, but the seventh day is a sabbath of rest, a
> day of sacred assembly. You are not to do any work; wherever you
> live, it is a Sabbath to the Lord'" (Leviticus 23:1–3).

It might surprise some to see a discussion of the biblical
holidays start with Shabbat. After all, this is such a common
day. It occurs once a week. The Jewish perspective is different.
It is not that Shabbat is so common, but that it is so special,
that we are to observe it every seven days. With that in mind,
it is perfectly logical to mention the Sabbath at the head of
the list. Besides, in the chronology of Leviticus 23, Shabbat
comes first.

Shabbat means "to rest," which tells us a large part of the purpose of this important observance—restoration. From the ancient Greeks to the modern corporate executive, mankind tends to become obsessed with work and "getting ahead." There is always more to do. Yet, without proper rest and refreshment, human strength and creativity fail.

In his infinite wisdom, God told the children of Israel to recharge themselves physically, emotionally and spiritually. God demonstrated this principle when he created the universe. For six days he formed the world and everything in it; but, on the seventh day he rested. Consequently, the seventh day, Shabbat, is to be a perpetual reminder of God the creator and our need to find rest in him (Exodus 31:16–17).

Based on the creation account of Genesis, Shabbat lasts from sundown Friday evening to sundown Saturday. God defines a day in the following order: "there was evening, and there was morning." Hence, the Hebrew calendar traditionally starts a day at sunset of the previous evening.

Some Christians might call Sunday the "Christian Sabbath"; however, this is technically incorrect. Sunday is never called the Sabbath in the Bible. In fact, the word "Sunday" never appears in the original text of the Scriptures. It is called "the first day of the week" (see Matthew 28:1 and I Corinthians 16:2, NIV). This is the biblical way of reckoning days of the week. All days are counted in relationship to Shabbat (first day, second day, etc.), giving further evidence of the centrality of this day to Jewish people.

## TRADITIONAL JEWISH OBSERVANCE

The traditional Jewish community understands the observance of Shabbat on many different levels. To the classical rabbis, verses such as Exodus 20:8 were to be eminently practical as we "remember the Sabbath day by keeping it holy." The implications of this verse have filled volumes of rabbinic commentaries, but the two-fold theme is clear: remember the creator and set the day aside to rest in him. Many beautiful Jewish customs have developed to remind people of these truths.

Preparation for Shabbat actually begins early Friday afternoon. Since it is a holy day, the most festive linens and silverware decorate the dinner table. It is customary to serve the finest meal of the week on the evening of Shabbat to emphasize its special quality.

Two candlesticks are set on the table, or in another prominent place. They symbolize the two-fold commandment to remember and sanctify. These candles are lit, according to rabbinic interpretation, eighteen minutes before sunset so that the act itself will not be considered work on the Sabbath. The Hebrew blessings are normally said by the woman of the house, though anyone may perform this duty. With a scarf covering her head, the woman lights the candles. She then circles her arms around in a motion as if to draw in the warmth of the light. Next she repeats the following blessings:

*Barukh atah Adonai Elohenu melekh ha-olam, asher kidshanu b'mitzvohtav v'tzi-vanu l'hadleek ner shel Shabbat.*

*Blessed art thou, O Lord our God, King of the universe, who has set us apart by your commandments and has commanded us to kindle the Sabbath lights.*

At this point, the woman closes her eyes for a moment of silent prayer. This also serves a good rabbinic purpose. If no work is to be done on Shabbat, how can the candles be lit? Rabbis say Shabbat does not start until the woman opens her eyes to see the lit candles; hence, the necessary time of prayer.

With the candles lit, the family now says the blessing over the wine or grape juice, which is in a special *kiddush* cup, a cup of sanctification. The fruit of the vine has always symbolized the joy of God's provisions in our everyday lives (Psalm 104:15). This may be a single cup or all those present at the table may have their own. As the cups are raised, the man of the house (if applicable) leads the group in the following blessing:

*Barukh atah Adonai Elohenu melekh ha-olam, boray p'ree ha-gahfen.*

*Blessed art thou, O Lord our God, King of the universe, who creates the fruit of the vine.*

Next comes the blessing over the *challah*, the twisted egg-bread which is traditional for the occasion. Normally there are two loaves. They represent the double portion of manna provided before every Sabbath to the Israelites in the wilderness. These are placed on a decorative "challah plate" and covered by a special cloth, which represents the dew that fell with the manna. The leader at the table now removes the challah cover, holds the plate for all to see and chants the following:

*Barukh atah Adonai Elohenu melekh ha-olam, ha-motzee lekhem meen ha-aretz.*

*Blessed art Thou, O Lord our God, King of the universe, who brings forth bread from the earth.*

The bread is usually broken by hand, not sliced with a knife. The idea is to symbolize the day when all weapons of war will be done away with at the coming of Messiah (Isaiah 2:4). A portion of bread is shared with each member at the table. Some people salt the challah to symbolize the salt on the sacrifices in the Temple era.

As the bread is shared by all, greetings of "Shabbat Shalom" (peaceful sabbath) are given to one another, often with a kiss or hug.

A final blessing is given before the actual meal—the prayer over the children. The father places his hand on the head of his son and says:

*Y'simkha Elohim k'Ephrayeem v'kheeM'nasheh.*

*May God make you like Ephraim and Manasseh (Genesis 48:20).*

For daughters, he gives a slightly different blessing:

*Y'simekh Elohim k'Sarah, Rivkah, Rakhel v'Leah.*

*May you be like Sarah, Rebekah, Rachel and Leah.*

The wife is also blessed, by reading *aishet khayeel*—the virtuous woman of Proverbs 31:10–31.

Shabbat is meant to be a wonderful time of worship to the Lord God and a time of family sharing.

The festival dinner is now served and leisurely table fellowship is enjoyed by all. For a change, no one is in a hurry. Even after dinner, many tradition *z'mirot* (songs) are sung, including the grace after dinner in Hebrew. Most synagogues have an Erev Shabbat (Sabbath eve) service.

On Saturday morning, preparations are made to attend the main synagogue service. An important part of Shabbat observance is attending corporate worship services. Since the days of Moses, these services have been held in the Tabernacle and Temple in order to fulfill the command to have a "sacred assembly" (holy convocation) to the Lord (Leviticus 23:3). With the destruction of the Temple, this practice has continued in the synagogues of the dispersion.

Shabbat not only provides the Jewish people with a time of rest, but allows corporate focus on the creator, the God of Israel.

The typical service, while having flexibility, has followed the same basic structure since the days of Ezra and Nehemiah (Nehemiah 8). There are opening praise psalms and hymns largely based on the Book of Psalms, along with later rabbinic readings. This is followed by the public reading/chanting from the scrolls of the Torah (Law) and *Haftorah* (Prophets). These readings are based on an annual or triennial cycle of selected passages. A third major section of the service is a sermon on the passage for that week.

After a closing hymn, the service ends with the *Oneg Shabbat* (Delight of the Sabbath), consisting of a small amount of wine or grape juice along with other refreshments. This custom is based on the passage in the prophets where Israel is told to "call the sabbath a delight." What better symbolism than a tasty treat? After the oneg, most people go home for lunch and spend the afternoon visiting friends or resting.

Much of the liturgy each week is standardized. However, there are additional blessings chanted once a month for Rosh Chodesh (New Moon), a special holiday related to Shabbat. In biblical times this was evidently an important feast to remind the Israelites of the cyclical nature of life (I Samuel 20:5; Isaiah 1:13, 66:23). Time marches on to its goal; therefore, we should number our days to walk in wisdom (Psalm 90:12).

Since the Jewish month starts with the New Moon, it became customary to bless God on the preceding Shabbat for the new month he provided. In modern synagogue observance, Rosh Chodesh is not a Sabbath itself. It is simply remembered by some additions in the liturgy such as the following:

> *May it be thy will, O Lord our God and God of our fathers, to renew unto us this coming month for our good and for blessing....The New Month of _____ will begin on _____.*
> *May the Holy One, blessed be he, renew this month for us and for all his people, the house of Israel, for life and peace, for gladness and joy, for salvation and comfort; and let us say, "Amen"* (*Sabbath And Festival Prayer Book*, p.129).

Because Shabbat is considered so special, there is not only a special start on Friday evening, but also a special close on Saturday evening. To distinguish Shabbat from all other days, rabbis created a service called *Havdalah* (Hebrew for "separated"). This is a simple service consisting of some interesting symbolic elements.

First a braided Havdalah candle is lit. This reminds us that the light of Shabbat will soon depart. The traditional verse read is Isaiah 12:2, "Surely God is my salvation." In Hebrew salvation is "yeshua".

A *b'sameem* (spice) box is passed around. Each person shakes the box and sniffs the sweet spices inside to remember the sweetness of the departing Sabbath. A cup of wine or grape juice is passed around the table, and after the traditional blessing is made, each person takes a sip. Then the candle is extinguished in the drops remaining in the cup.

The Havdalah service closes with the singing of a significant song. *Eliyahu Ha-Navi* (Elijah The Prophet). It is strongly messianic in content. "May Elijah come with Messiah, Son of David." At sunset Saturday evening the new week begins. Having enjoyed the refreshing rest and worship of Shabbat, it is appropriate to consider the ultimate fulfillment of Shabbat, when Messiah will come with his kingdom of peace and rest.

## SHABBAT IN THE NEW TESTAMENT

Because of its centrality in Jewish tradition, we would naturally expect to find the observance of Shabbat mentioned throughout the New Testament. Much of the Shabbat synagogue service is derived from Nehemiah 8. However, the most detailed account in Scripture of such a service is found in the Gospels.

> Now when he went to Natzaret, where he had been brought up, on Shabbat he went to the synagogue as usual. He stood up to read, and he was given the scroll of the prophet Yesha'yahu. Unrolling the scroll, he found the place where it was written, "The Spirit of Adonai is upon me; therefore he has anointed me to announce Good News to the poor; he has sent me to proclaim freedom for the imprisoned and renewed sight for the blind, to release those who have been crushed, to proclaim a year of the favor of Adonai."

> After closing the scroll and returning it to the shammash, he sat down; and the eyes of everyone in the synagogue were fixed on him. He started to speak to them: "Today, as you heard it read, this passage of the Tanakh was fulfilled (Luke 4:16–21).

The first-century synagogue service is described with amazing detail in this passage. Notice the reading from the Torah and Haftorah scrolls by a special reader. Yeshua read from the Haftorah portion that Shabbat as he turned to Isaiah 61, an obvious messianic section. The last reader was customarily given the honor of expounding on the reading with a sermon. And what a sermon it was! Yeshua claimed to be the very Messiah promised to fulfill this ministry.

There was mixed response to such a controversial sermon. Some people were "speaking well of him" (v. 22) while others were "filled with fury" (v. 28). The message of Yeshua, even today, brings controversy. Either he was a great deceiver or he is the Mashiach, the anointed one, who fulfills the Hebrew Scriptures. For many people today, both Jews and Gentiles, his words ring with the truth of God!

Yeshua made it his habit to worship at the weekly Shabbat service. What else would he do? He was born a Jew and lived a life consistent with much of traditional Judaism of his day. Likewise, the first Jewish disciples continued in the traditional forms of synagogue worship. (See Acts 13:13 and 18:4 for examples.)

This does not imply that Yeshua agreed with every detail or every rabbinic attitude of Sabbath observance. Indeed, he tried to correct imbalances in rabbinic perspective by reminding the people "Shabbat was made for mankind, not mankind for Shabbat" (Mark 2:27).

Sadly, too often the people forgot to make Shabbat a delight, relegating it to a list of rules instead. Yeshua challenged the people of his day to remain biblically balanced, to enter into the true rest of God's spirit. This same appeal goes forth in this generation.

## THE PROPHETIC FULFILLMENT

The prophetic fulfillment of Shabbat is summarized in the New Testament book "Hebrews," or "Messianic Jews." It was written to the Messianic Jews of the first century:

*So there remains a Shabbat-keeping for God's people. For the one who has entered God's rest has also rested from his own works, as God did from his"* (Hebrews 4:9–10).

Spiritual rest is the prophetic fulfillment of the biblical observance of Shabbat. The seventh day (Shabbat) is a wonderful reminder of a coming day set aside to rest in the Messiah. The 1000 year Kingdom of Yeshua will be a beautiful time of rest and corporate worship of the King. May it come soon! In the meantime, Messiah bids us to experience the truth of Shabbat in our daily walk: "Come to me, all of you who are struggling and burdened, and I will give you rest" (Matthew 11:28). As we celebrate Shabbat, may spiritual rest in Yeshua constantly be our experience!

## A Practical Guide for Believers in Messiah

There are many wonderful lessons from Shabbat to be enjoyed by followers of Yeshua. As with all the feasts, the most important element is the spirit in which we observe the holy days. Many practical expressions of Shabbat observance were meant to illustrate the rest and refreshment God offers his people. Messianic believers fully appreciate this rest by abiding in Messiah.

As believers in Messiah, Shabbat can be observed in a multitude of ways, depending on one's convictions and desires. Late Friday afternoon may be set aside to prepare for the day of rest (Luke 23:54). As sunset approaches the family gathers, dressed in festive attire, for the blessings to welcome Shabbat and sanctify the meal. (See traditional blessings above.)

Messianic Jews and Messianic Gentiles may want to modify the traditional blessing with a more specifically messianic one. Over the candles, the following may be said:

*Barukh atah Adonai Elohenu melekh ha-olam, asher kidshanu b'mitzvohtav l'hayot or l'goyeem v'natan-lanu Yeshua m'sheekhaynu ha-or la-olam.*

*Blessed art thou, O Lord Our God, King of the universe, who has
sanctified us by thy commandments and commanded us to be
a light unto the nations and has given us Yeshua, the light of the
world.*

Next, the blessings over the wine and bread are chanted.
The traditional blessings are consistent with faith in Yeshua
and should suffice for the kiddush and motzi (see above).
Likewise, the beautiful Scripture blessings for the wife (Proverbs 31) and for the children (Genesis 48:20) can be wonderful
focal points of the Erev Shabbat dinner.

At this point the festival dinner is served with all the best
trimmings, enhancing the special nature of this holy day.
Dinner may be followed by a joyous time of family fellowship
and singing some traditional or messianic songs. All the
customs are reminders of the complete rest we have found in
Messiah Yeshua (Matthew 11:28).

There may be a messianic congregation in your area that
has Shabbat services. Many have a Friday night Erev Shabbat
service, which is a meaningful way to come together as the
corporate family of God.

Most messianic groups have a Saturday morning Shabbat
service. There are compelling reasons for this since this is
traditionally the service where the Torah scroll is read. It may
also be a more manageable time to have a children's Shabbat
school program. Whatever the schedule, the Scriptures exhort
to "not neglect our own congregational meetings for worship,
instruction and fellowship (Hebrews 10:25; Leviticus 23:3). If
there is no messianic synagogue in your area, why not consider
celebrating the feast at home with other interested families?

There are some good ways to continue in the spirit of
Shabbat after the Saturday morning service. Perhaps a lunch
with the family or friends would create an opportunity to
develop deeper spiritual friendships. In the spirit of rest,
many prefer to nap and relax for the afternoon. In our fast-
paced society people need a time for recharging their physical
and spiritual batteries.

Messianic modifications may be incorporated into the Havdalah service, but no changes need to be made to the traditional service (see above). The Havdalah candle and spices serve as a graphic reminder of the coming day when Messiah Yeshua will establish his true Shabbat light and the sweetness of his coming kingdom! May we, his followers, appreciate the foretaste of this truth as we observe this rich holy day, Shabbat.

# Shabbat Recipes

## MAIN DISH CHICKEN

**Ingredients:**
Up to 4 lbs. chicken pieces, can remove skin.
1/4 cup flour
1/4 teaspoon salt
1/16 teaspoon pepper
1/4 cup olive or salad oil
1 small sliced onion
1 sliced clove garlic
3 or 4 chopped celery stalks
1 medium-sized carrot
1 1/2 cups hot chicken broth
1 cup sliced sauteed mushrooms

**Directions:**
Mix flour, salt and pepper in a plastic bag. Place 1 or 2 chicken peices in bag, close and shake vigorously. Repeat until all pieces are coated. In a large skillet, brown the pieces in oil. Remove the pieces and place them in a casserole dish that is large enough to lay them out singly.

In the remaining oil, cook the onion, garlic, celery and carrot for 10 minutes. Place the vegetables over the chicken. Pour the broth on top. Cover and bake at 350° for 1 1/2 hours or until tender. Place the mushrooms on top during the last 5 minutes of baking.

## SHABBAT CAKE

**Ingredients:**
2 1/2 cups sugar
1 cup oil
1 teaspoon vanilla
4 eggs
3 cups flour
1 teaspoon baking powder
2 teaspoons baking soda
1 cup cocoa, either baking or sweetened drink mix
   (baking chocolate makes a heavier cake)
2 cups liquid coffee

**Directions:**
Mix the sugar, oil, vanilla and eggs. Gradually add in the other dry ingredients, finishing with the liquid coffee. The batter will be very liquid. Bake at 350° for 45 minutes in greased bunt pan or 2 loaf pans. Check with a toothpick. Cool thoroughly before removing from pan.

## CHOPPED LIVER

**Ingredients:**
1 lb. chicken livers
1 large onion, chopped
4 hard boiled eggs, sliced
oil

**Directions:**
Heat oil in a large skillet. Add the livers. Cook 3 minutes and turn over. Place onion on top and cook 1 minute more. Cut into the livers to check if they are cooked. Flip so that onions are underneath and cook until onions are translucent. Using a slotted spoon, place the liver, onion and eggs through a food processor until you have a spreadable mixture. Can season sparingly with garlic power. Serve with bread, matzah or crackers.

## AUNT SARA'S CHALLAH (SABBATH BREAD)

**Ingredients:**
1 cake fresh yeast
1/4 cup warm water
5 cups flour
1 teaspoon salt
1 tablespoon sugar
1 tablespoon salad oil
1 egg beaten
warm water

*Glaze:*
1 egg yolk diluted with 1 teaspoon water
poppy seed or sesame seed (optional)

**Directions:**

Soften yeast in 1/4 cup warm water. Sift together dry ingredients. Add oil. Add softened yeast and beaten egg. Mix thoroughly, adding just enough water for smooth kneading. Knead well. Place in a bowl and cover with a tea towel. Let stand until it "bubbles." Knead again. Cover; let rise until doubled in bulk. Divide dough into three equal parts. Roll into three strips and braid them. Place in a baking pan and let rise until doubled in bulk. Just before baking, brush with diluted egg yolk. Sprinkle with poppy seed or sesame seed if desired. Bake at 350° for about an hour until golden brown.

• Note: This recipe is from Love and Knishes, a Jewish cookbook written by the author's relative, Sara Kasdan. See Bibliography.

# Shabbat Crafts

## HEAD COVERINGS

### Boys:

A *kippah* is a circular head covering for boys. A bobby pin or hair clip is necessary for it to stay on well. If plain kippahs are available for you to buy and decorate, wonderful! If not, you may sew one together. It can then be decorated with markers, fabric paint, sew-on or iron-on trims.

Cut four pieces like the shape below. Using a 1/4-inch seam allowance, sew two pieces together along the edges to make double layers. Repeat with the other two pieces. *Then* sew both double pieces together along the edges. Finish the bottom, enclosing in seam tape and sewing.

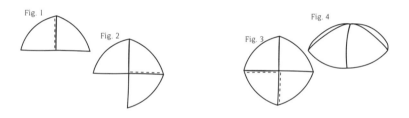

Fig. 1   Fig. 2   Fig. 3   Fig. 4

**Girls:**

An easy covering is made by cutting lace into a large rectangle, 32 to 36 inches wide or as wide as the selvage allows, by 15 inches. This doesn't give girls much to decorate. However, a light fabric like muslin could be cut and edges finished as the boys. Designs (like the one below) could be traced on the covering. Themes could include doves, Shabbat Shalom, Jewish stars, and so on.

## CHALLAH COVERS

Cut rectangles out of a white or light-colored fabric. Muslin is good, or white sheets. The size of the cover depends on the size of fabric available. Dimensions may vary from a minimum of 14 by 17 inches to 18 by 20 inches. Finish the edges of the fabric. Rolling the edges and sewing them is the most durable finish. Make enlarged copies of the four designs on the following pages.

Give each child a design sheet. Tape this to a table and center the cloth over it and tape it down also. The design should be traced using crayons. The children should color in the designs completely. Then an adult will iron the wax off by placing a heavy gauge paper towel over the design and ironing until the wax is absorbed onto the towel. Be sure to not use too high of a temperature setting.

Challah Cover Pattern #1

Challah Cover Pattern #2

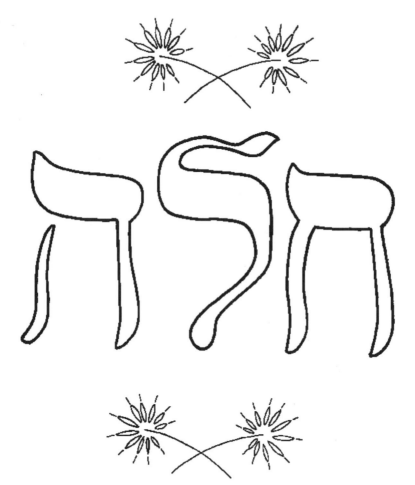

These Hebrew letters mean *Challah*.

Challah Cover Pattern #3

These Hebrew words say *Shabbat Shalom*.

Challah Cover Pattern #4

*Shabbat Shalom* means "Have a good Sabbath."

## CANDLESTICKS

**Materials:**
2 pieces of wood about 6 inches long
wooden rings (big enough for candles to fit into)
wood glue
glitter
paint
markers
glue.

**Directions:**
Glue wooden rings onto wood base and decorate.

## KIDDUSH CUP

**Materials:**
frozen juice concentrate cans
colored paper
markers
clear contact paper
stickers—optional

**Directions:**
Cut colored paper rectangles that will fit around the empty can. Decorate. Tape the decorated paper onto the can and cover with contact paper.

# Shabbat Music

## Shabbat Shalom

*Translation:*
Peaceful Sabbath

## SONGS FOR HAVDALAH

# Behold God Is My Salvation   *(Isaiah 12:2)*

By Stuart Dauermann
Used by permission
Integrated Copyright Group

# Eliyahu Ha-navi

*Liturgy*

*Folk Song*

D.C. al Fine

*Translation:*
May the prophet Elijah come soon, in our time, with the Messiah, son of David.

# 2

# Pesach and Hag HaMatzah
## Passover and the Feast of Unleavened Bread

## THE HISTORICAL BACKGROUND

*The Lord's Passover begins at twilight on the fourteenth day of the first month. On the fifteenth day of that month the Lord's Feast of Unleavened Bread begins; for seven days you must eat bread made without yeast. On the first day hold a sacred assembly and do no regular work. For seven days present an offering made to the Lord by fire. And on the seventh day hold a sacred assembly and do no regular work* (Leviticus 23:5–8).

25

The holy day, Pesach (Passover), announces the arrival of spring on the Jewish calendar. Its importance to the biblical plan can be seen in the timing of the festival. As one looks at the major holy days in Scripture, a striking parallel can be seen. Major days are bunched in two groups in two different times of the year. The spring holy days of Passover and the Feast of Unleavened Bread, First Fruits and Pentecost occur within a fifty-day time span from March to June. A long summer intervenes until the fall holy days of Rosh HaShanah, Yom Kippur and Sukkot, usually in September and/or October. The chronology of these days perfectly fits the salvation plan of God through his Messiah, Yeshua of Nazareth as you will see.

The meaning of Passover is found in Leviticus 23. The Hebrew word "pesach" means "to spring, jump or pass over" something; hence the English name, Passover. This is a historical reference to God's deliverance of Israel from the bondage of Egypt as recorded in Exodus.

Because of the increasing hardness of Pharaoh's heart, God had to send ten plagues to persuade the blinded leader to let Israel go. As devastating as the first nine plagues were, it wasn't until the tenth and final plague that Pharaoh acquiesced to the God of Israel. In this judgment, God said he would send the Angel of Death over the land of Egypt to take the firstborn boy of every household.

With every judgment of God there is also a way of escape. Any household that put the blood of the sacrificial lamb on its doorpost was given a special promise: "...when I see the blood, I will pass over you. No destructive plague will touch you..." (Exodus 12:13).

Passover clearly typifies redemption in a dramatic way. It is a holy day commemorating God's deliverance of Israel from the slavery of Egypt. Yet Pesach also holds a greater prophetic picture of God's plan for world redemption.

### TRADITIONAL JEWISH OBSERVANCE

Because of its historical meaning for the Jewish people, the celebration of Passover is perhaps the most elaborate feast. The Torah says the people should remove any leavened products from their households (Exodus 12:15). This was to remind them that they had to flee Egypt so quickly that the bread in their ovens did not have time to rise. Every spring, in Jewish homes, a furious housecleaning takes place to remove any leavened products before Passover begins.

After cleaning the home, preparation for the central tradition associated with the day, the Passover *seder* meal, occurs. Seder means "order" of the service. This is based on the directives given in Exodus 12. God told the Israelites the evening shall be commemorated by eating three things: lamb, *matzah* (unleavened bread) and bitter herbs.

Rabbis later added numerous other elements, including green vegetables, a roasted egg, *kharoset* (apple/nut mix) and four cups of wine. These are arranged on a ceremonial seder plate, and the cups are sipped from a decorative kiddush cup (wine goblet).

Later in history rabbis added a fifth cup called the Cup of Elijah. This particular cup is filled with the hope that the prophet Elijah will come, drink from the cup and announce that the Messiah has come (Malachi 4:5). Passover, like most of the biblical holy days, features special, meaningful foods. All this reminds us that, from a Jewish perspective, theology is not only taught, it is also eaten. This is one more reason I believe all people—Jews and Gentiles, adults and children— can learn so much by celebrating the feasts.

A particularly intriguing element incorporated by rabbis is called the *matzah tash*. This is a linen pouch or plate with three different sections. A piece of matzah is placed within each section, individually set apart yet united in the one container. Rabbinic commentaries don't give the exact origin of this custom. They speculate that the matzah tash represents unity—perhaps the unity of the people of Israel through the forefathers (Abraham, Isaac and Jacob) or the unity of the families of Israel (Aaron, the Levites, the common people).

During the first part of the seder, the middle piece of matzah is taken out and broken in half. Half of the matzah is placed back in the matzah tash. The other half is wrapped in a napkin and hidden somewhere in the room by the leader of the seder. The hidden matzah is called the *afikomen*, a Greek word meaning "that which comes last." Rabbis say it alludes to the fact that the afikomen is the last thing tasted at the seder, the dessert. Others have suggested the translation "he will come again." This sense of the word has much meaning to the Messianic believer since it pictures the resurrection and return of Messiah.

A structured order of service was developed into the *Haggadah*, a booklet that retells the history and significance of Pesach. The Passover seder is a ceremonial dinner centered around reading the Haggadah. Most Jewish communities outside Israel celebrate the seder the first two nights of Pesach (the 15th and 16th of the Hebrew month of *Nisan*).

Pesach lasts eight days, and during this time no leavened foods are to be eaten. The Scriptures indicate that the seven subsequent days are an entirely independent feast called "Unleavened Bread" (Leviticus 23:6). Modern observance has combined these two feasts into one eight-day festival called Pesach. Through the symbolism and celebration, Jewish families are reminded of the great redemption of the first Passover.

## NEW TESTAMENT OBSERVANCE

Most of this tradition was fully developed before the first century. It is not surprising to see numerous references to Passover in the New Covenant. Passover is mentioned in the Gospel accounts (see Luke 2:41 and John 5:1, 6:4), as well as the book of Acts (see Acts 12:3–4). By far the most famous account is the last Passover celebrated by Yeshua and his Jewish disciples in an upper room (Matthew 26 and Luke 22). In these passages one sees the traditions of the first century, and some spiritual lessons taught by the Messiah.

Among the traditional items mentioned are the lamb (Luke 22:8), bitter herbs (Matthew 26:23), the washings (John

13:1–15), the four cups of wine (Matthew 26 and Luke 22) and matzah (Matthew 26:26). The lamb reminds one of the means of redemption, the blood of the sacrifice. In this case, Messiah became our Pesach (John 1:29). The bitter herbs speak of terrible bondage to an oppressor. Not surprisingly, it was in the bowl of bitter herbs that Judas, a man who came to a bitter end, dipped his matzah. The hand and foot washings typify the need for cleansing before approaching a holy God.

Each of the four cups of wine teaches an important lesson. According to ancient rabbis, these four cups are based on the four promises given to the children of Israel in Exodus 6:6–7:

> Therefore, say to the Israelites, "I am the Lord and I will bring you out from under the yoke of the Egyptian. I will free you from being slaves to them and will redeem you with an outstretched arm and with mighty acts of judgment. I will take you as my own people, and I will be your God...

The Cup of Sanctification appears at the start of the Seder. How appropriate to sanctify, or set apart, this service as special to the Lord. The second cup is known as the Cup of Praise (sometimes called the Cup of Plagues) because we must praise the Holy One who has done such great things. The third Cup, the Cup of Redemption, was designated by Messiah Yeshua as a special memorial through all generations. It was once a memorial cup of physical redemption for the Jews from Egypt. For believers in Yeshua this cup symbolizes the spiritual redemption found in Messiah's sacrifice.

How often one should celebrate the "Lord's supper" has been debated. The key phrase for understanding the answer is contained in I Corinthians 11:26: "For as often as you eat this bread and drink the cup, you proclaim the death of the Lord, until he comes."

Some churches interpret this to mean as often as you drink a ceremonial cup. That could be every Sunday, once a month or any other designated time of celebration. My personal view is that the most natural interpretation from the context is to partake of the cup every Passover. The emphasis, according to this view, should be on the phrase "do this," meaning the unleavened bread and third cup of Passover.

Our messianic congregation celebrates the Lord's supper every year at our Passover seder. This cup may be celebrated more often; but there is not a more appropriate time to celebrate the message of redemption than at the feast of redemption.

The Cup of Acceptance, or Praise, is the fourth cup, and a fitting close to the Seder service. After Sanctification, Praise or Plagues, and Redemption, this cup reveals the wonderful symbolic truth of God accepting his people. It is around this cup that some of the Hallel psalms are sung.

## THE PROPHETIC FULFILLMENT

After exploring the background of Pesach, the prophetic fulfillment of this holy day is clear. It can best be summed up by the word "redemption." Rabbi Saul of Tarsus (the apostle Paul) states this theme beautifully and succinctly in his letter to the Corinthian believers. They were told to deal with moral problems within their members. To make his point, Paul draws upon the well-understood analogy of Pesach:

> Your boasting is not good. Don't you know the saying, "It takes only a little chametz to leaven a whole batch of dough? Get rid of the old chametz, so that you can be a new batch of dough, because in reality you are unleavened. For our Pesach lamb, the Messiah, has been sacrificed. So let us celebrate the seder, not with leftover chametz, the chametz of wickedness and evil, but with the matzah of purity and truth (I Corinthians 5:6–8).

Slaying the lamb at Passover foreshadowed the greater redemption found in God's appointed lamb, the Messiah. What a special joy to celebrate this feast of redemption (as encouraged by Paul), for those who have truly experienced redemption in Yeshua HaMashiach, the savior of the world!

## A PRACTICAL GUIDE FOR BELIEVERS IN MESSIAH

Many previously described customs can be meaningful when observed by followers of Yeshua. Those who desire to enter into the full celebration of the holy day begin before the arrival of the seder by cleansing all leaven from the house. Floors are swept, vacuumed and mopped. Cupboards are cleared of leavened products and cleaned. Pots and dishes are thoroughly washed to remove any possible fragments of leaven. The spirit of the law is to remove all leaven from our houses (Exodus 12:19–20). This is also symbolic of the spiritual cleansing of our hearts (I Corinthians 5:6–8).

My suggestion, in that spirit of freedom, is to adapt the preparation to a comfortable degree. For some, this may mean all of the above cleaning. For others, it may mean a cursory cleaning to merely symbolize the truth of Passover. Let every person be convinced in his own mind (Romans 14).

After a general cleaning in the first weeks of Nisan, the attention becomes more focused as the day of Pesach approaches. After sundown on the fourteenth of Nisan, a special ceremony called *bedikat khameytz* (the search for the leaven) takes place in the home. The last little bits of leaven are found and removed from the premises.

The details of this process are intriguing. Since the house has previously been cleaned, the leader of the house must purposely hide some leaven (bits of cookie or bread) in various places. Then the leader takes a feather, a wooden spoon and a lighted candle, and the family begins searching for the final leaven. This can be a great time to get children involved because it is like a game of hide-and-seek.

The spiritual lessons are quite striking, however. The leaven (sin) must be cleansed from our dwellings (and hearts). The method itself is informative. The light of the candle (the Word of God) illumines our sin (Psalm 119:11). The leaven is scooped onto the wooden spoon for removal (like the wooden cross of the Messiah). The following morning, this last bit of collected leaven is burnt outside the home (in a can or bag) to symbolize its final destruction. This symbolizes Messiah's destroying sin "outside the camp," and making freedom from the power of sin available for all who believe.

These customs may seem strange to the uninitiated, but the deep spiritual truth will be evident to discerning believers in Yeshua. Even something as unusual as bedikat khameytz can become a meaningful ceremony for those whose hearts have been cleansed by the Messiah.

On the day of 14 Nisan, as the first day of Passover approaches, final preparations for the seder must be made. By now, the preliminary arrangements, such as shopping for "Kosher For Passover" products (matzah, wine or grapejuice, and any other unleavened food substitutes) should be completed.

A traditional seder plate and ceremonial items will also be needed. The *zeroah* is a lamb shankbone representing the lamb sacrifice. If no lamb shankbone is available, a turkey or chicken bone that has been roasted by fire may be substituted.

The *baytzah* is a roasted, hardboiled egg representing the burnt offerings of the Temple period. The *maror* (bitter herbs) is usually horseradish, which is a reminder of the bitterness of slavery to sin. *Kharoset* (the sweet apple/nut mix) is a wonderful reminder of the sweetness of our redemption. The *karpas* (parsley), a green vegetable, speaks of life. All these seder plate elements can be purchased or prepared from the recipes included later in this chapter.

A kiddush cup (goblet) for each person plus the cup of Elijah with its own placesetting is also needed to prepare the seder table. A matzah tash and ceremonial washing bowl of water are also essential items.

Each reading participant will need a haggadah. If the leader feels comfortable, it is possible to use a traditional haggadah available through any Jewish bookstore. Many believers prefer to use a messianic Jewish haggadah. These contain most of the traditional readings, but are also accompanied by relevant New Covenant passages and explanations.

One resource I recommend to messianic believers is *The Messianic Passover Haggadah* by Messianic Jewish Publishers. It is a quality messianic haggadah. Messianic Jewish Publishers also has a very helpful preparation guide for the seder meal.

Pesach officially arrives as the sun sets on the 15th of Nisan. Since most Jewish communities outside Israel celebrate the first two nights of Passover with a traditional seder, many messianic believers have different types of seders each night.

Our congregational custom is to have a large community seder the first night of Pesach for our members, and to reach out to those who need to hear the message of redemption. The second night is usually spent at a smaller, home seder with family and close friends. Whatever your options, I encourage you to make plans to celebrate this wonderful festival!

The seder is the focal point of the celebration of Passover, yet it is an eight-day holy day. The Torah says we are to remove the leaven from our homes and eat matzah during this time. For some, this might be the ultimate inconvenience. What? No bagels for eight days? Yet, when spiritually appraised, even something like eating matzah crackers for a week can be an uplifting experience.

Remember the symbolism. It is not just spring house-cleaning; it is to remind us of our need for spiritual cleansing and repentance. Hence, every time we eat a matzah sandwich during Pesach, we are reminded of the meaning of the holy day. Every time we long for a leavened cookie we are reminded of this great spiritual truth?

It is my prayer that Pesach will become a source of joyful celebration as believers experience Messiah our Passover in an intimate and practical way. Let us therefore celebrate the feast (I Corinthians 5:8).

# Recipes for Passover

As you might imagine, after some 3500 years of observing the Passover, the Jewish community has become pretty creative in its celebration. We have found 1001 ways to use matzah in our regular meals. Recipes for the Passover Seder meal can be found in the guide published by Lederer Messianic Ministries. Here are some of our favorites to help make the remainder of Pesach a little more tasty.

For breakfasts, Matzah Pancakes can be made by using 1 cup of matzah meal, 1 cup milk and 3 eggs to form a batter. The pancakes (like everything else at Pesach) are heavier than your normal buttermilk variety.

Matza Brie, the Passover equivalent to French Toast, is made by softening matzahs in water, squeezing the liquid out, then breaking the matzahs into a mixture of beaten eggs and a small amount of milk. This is then fried until the egg mixture is cooked through. This can be eaten with sugar, jams or syrup. Some people eat it with salt and pepper.

A Kasdan tradition that is useful is what we call the "Egg McMatzah"...a little crunchy but not bad.

Lunch is a good time to eat a-la-carte. Hardboiled egg slices, salads, tuna, cheese wedges and fresh fruits can go a long way in filling the Passover menu. You can even try a number of matzah sandwiches with appropriate fillings. Look at it this way: you'll really appreciate the convenience of the fastfood hamburger at the end of the week!

Dinner suggestions include chicken and fish dishes. An interesting meal can be made by substituting matzah for noodles in a Lasagne recipe. This can be done by soaking whole matzahs for a short time in water then gently pressing the water out. Likewise, matzah meal can replace bread crumbs in a Meatloaf recipe.

Perhaps the most difficult part of the "fast" of Passover is surviving dessert and snacks. Not to worry! After 3500 years of matzah the Jewish people have come up with some pretty creative answers. You will find a number of desserts in the following recipes.

Above all, remember the meaning of Passover through all these foods. It is a time to clean out the leaven and to restore a pure walk with Messiah (I Corinthians 5:6–7). May every crunchy bite remind us of the spiritual beauty of the season!

## APPLE CAKE

### Ingredients:
    3 eggs
    3/4 cup sugar
    1/3 cup oil
    3/4 cup matzah cake meal
    5 apples, pared and thinly sliced
    1/3 cup walnuts
    1/2 cup sugar
    2 teaspoons cinnamon

### Directions:
Beat eggs with sugar and oil until the mixture is light. Add cake meal and mix well. Pour half of the batter into a lightly greased 8 or 9 inch square pan. Distribute half of the apples over the batter. Pour the remaining batter over the apples and cover with the remaining apples. Combine walnuts, sugar and cinnamon. Sprinkle over the apples. The recipe may be doubled and baked in a 9x13 inch pan at 350° for 1 1/2 hours.

## MOIST BROWNIES

### Ingredients:
    5 eggs
    1 cup margarine, melted
    3 cups sugar
    1 tablespoon vanilla
    8 oz. baking chocolate, melted
    1 1/2 cups matzah cake meal
    2 cups chopped walnuts

**Directions:**

Beat eggs, margarine, sugar and vanilla for a complete 10 minutes at a medium speed. Stir in the melted chocolate. Fold in the cake meal and beat minimally. Bake in a greased 9x13 inch pan at 375° for 35–40 minutes.

## APPLE MATZAH KUGEL

**Ingredients:**

4 matzahs
4 eggs, well beaten
1/2 teaspoon salt
3/4 cup sugar
3/8 cup (3 oz or 6 tablespoons) melted margarine
1 1/2 teaspoons cinnamon
3/4 cup chopped walnuts, optional
3 large apples, pared and chopped
3/4 cup raisins, golden are best

**Directions:**

Break matzahs into pieces; soak in water until soft. Drain, squeezing gently. Beat eggs with salt, sugar, margarine and cinnamon. Mix in matzah, apples, nuts and raisins. Bake in greased 1 1/2 quart dish at 350° for 45 minutes.

## CHOCOLATE CHIP COOKIE BARS

**Ingredients:**

2/3 cup margarine, melted
2 cups brown sugar
3 eggs
1 teaspoon vanilla
2 cups matzah cake flour
1/2 teaspoon salt
1/2 cup chopped wlnuts
3/4 cup chocolate chips

**Directions:**

Mix margarine, sugar eggs, vanilla, flour and salt. Mix in walnuts and chocolate chips. Press into a greased 9x13 inch pan. Bake at 350° for 25 minutes.

# Passover Crafts

## MATZAH HOLDER

### Materials:
Four fabric or felt squares (minimum 9 inches)
sewing machine
craft glue or glue gun
decorating pens
sequins
tassle or fringe.

### Directions:
Layer all four fabrics together and glue or sew around three sides leaving one side open for inserting the matzahs. Glue or paint or color designs on top. A fringe may be attached around the edge.

## SEDER PLATE

### Materials:
Large sturdy paper plates
circle cut-outs of seder elements
pens
glue
clear contact paper or cupcake papers (optional)

### Directions:
Color and cut out elements.
Glue onto plate and cover with contact paper for a useable plate. If plate is to be only decorative, place designs inside cupcake papers. Glue onto plate.

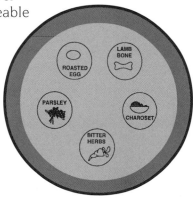

# Passover Music

## Dayenu

2. Elu Elu natan lanu et ha Torah, dayenu!
3. Elu Elu natan lanu et Yeshua, dayenu!*
*Translation:*
Had He taken us out of Egypt, it would have been sufficient!
Had He given us the Torah, it would have been sufficient!
Had He given us Yeshua, it would have been sufficient!*
*Third verse adapted by Messianic Jews*

## Eliyahu Ha-navi

*Translation:*
May the prophet Elijah come soon, in our time, with the Messiah, son of David.

# 3

# ■Sfirat HaOmer

## The Early First Fruits

### THE HISTORICAL BACKGROUND

The Lord said to Moses, "Speak to the Israelites and say to them: 'When you enter the land I am going to give to you and you reap its harvest, bring to the priest a sheaf of the first grain you harvest. He is to wave the sheaf before the Lord so it will be accepted on your behalf; the priest is to wave it on the day after the Sabbath. On the day you wave the sheaf, you must sacrifice as a burnt offering to the Lord a lamb a year old without defect, together with its grain offering of two-tenths of an ephah of fine flour mixed with oil—an offering made to the Lord by fire, a pleasing aroma—and its drink offering of a fourth of a hin of wine. You must not *eat any bread, or roasted new grain, until the very day you bring this offering to your God. This is to be a lasting ordinance for the generations to come, wherever you live'"* (Leviticus 23:9–14).

The series of spring holy days continues with the arrival of *Sfirat HaOmer*, First Fruits, sometimes called Yom HaBikkurim. Since it comes on the heels of the major festival, Passover, First Fruits is often overlooked. We shall see, however, that this biblical holy day observance should be one of the more important of all the festivals for Messianic Jews *and* Gentiles.

The meaning of this holy day is understood in its name. Sfirat HaOmer literally means "the Counting of the Sheaf." It speaks of the earliest harvest that takes place in Israel, the barley harvest. Like the fall holy day, Sukkot, this festival emphasizes the agrarian culture of the ancient Middle East.

In practical terms, Sfirat HaOmer was the first harvest of the spring and, as such, was the perfect time to make the grain offering to the Lord. As Leviticus states, this first of the barley harvest was to be brought as an offering to the priest in the Tabernacle/Temple. The lesson is clear: if God has been faithful to bless us with this early harvest, he will most certainly provide the harvest of later summer.

The Jewish observance of this festival has varied through-out history. In ancient practice, in the days of the Temple, it was quite an elaborate ceremony of bringing the offering as a thanksgiving tithe to God. The Talmud states that a priest would meet a group of Jewish pilgrims on the edge of the city and, from there, lead them up to the Temple mount. As they carried their offerings of the first fruits, the priest would lead a praise service with music, praise psalms and dance.

As the group of worshipers arrived at the Temple compound, the priest would take the sheaves, lift some in the air and wave them in every direction. By so doing, the whole crowd would be acknowledging God's provision and sovereignty over all the earth (see Edersheim, *The Temple*, p. 256 and following pages).

While the customs of the ancient festival are fairly straight-forward, a controversy developed as to when Sfirat HaOmer was to begin. The question was how to understand the starting point of the holiday as stated in the phrase "after the Sabbath" (Leviticus 23:11). To which Sabbath does this refer?

The two major schools of Jewish tradition in the first century were divided on the issue. The Sadducees (the aristocratic sect associated with the Temple service) believed it referred to the seventh-day Sabbath. Hence, the wave offering would be lifted up on the next day, the first day of the week.

The Pharisees (primarily the synagogue rabbis of the common people) saw it another way. They pointed out that given the context of the passage, Pesach is the Sabbath spoken of. Consequently, the day after the Sabbath of Passover would always fall on the 16th of Nisan, irrespective of what day of the week it was. This controversy continued to be debated, each group following its own convictions about the start of Sfirat HaOmer.

Not only were there disagreements between the rival Sadducees and Pharisees, but there were varying perspectives within the Pharisaic groups. Judean Pharisees disagreed with the Galilean Pharisees (see Hoehner, page 87). A final decision came in a rather unexpected way when the Temple was destroyed in the year 70 C.E. With the Sadducees suddenly unemployed, it was the synagogue service that became the focal point of the Jewish community. The Pharisees continued to thrive and their interpretation became accepted as the final authority; it remains so even to the present day.

## TRADITIONAL JEWISH OBSERVANCE

The modern synagogue observance of Sfirat HaOmer is not very complex. While in the Temple period it involved offerings, processions, and praise services, the contemporary celebration consists primarily of prayers and blessings from a Jewish prayer book. These help the people reflect on the symbolic meaning of the day, counting the days from the barley to the wheat harvest at Shavuot, Pentecost, the next holy day. Many Jews begin the counting of the omer on the second night of Passover, at their second Seder, with the reading of the traditional blessing:

*Barukh atah Adonai Elohenu melekh ha-olam, asher kidshanu b'mitzvohtav v'tzi-vanu al sfirat haomer.*

*Blessed art thou, O Lord our God, King of the universe, who has set us apart by your commandments and has commanded us concerning the counting of the sheaf.*

This blessing is read every evening for the next forty-nine days with an adjustment made according to the number of days that have been counted. For example:

*Ha-yom, yom echad l'omer. Today is the first day of the sheaf.*

The next day would be the second day, then the third, and so on until the forty-ninth day is reached. The fiftieth day marks the next major holy day on the biblical calendar, Shavuot (Pentecost). In essence then, Sfirat HaOmer is not a countdown but a countup in anticipation of the next great work of God at Shavuot. The blessings and numbering of the omer can be found in most Jewish prayer books. Some people even make use of a special calendar which helps keep track of the appropriate day.

Another aspect of the modern Jewish observance is that the Sfirat period of forty-nine days has become known as a time of semi-mourning. This is because a number of tragedies took place during this time of year. Most notable is a plague that struck the disciples of Rabbi Akiva in the second Roman revolt of 135 C.E. An exception to this time of semi-mourning is the thirty-third day of the omer, called in Hebrew "Lag B'Omer" (the Hebrew letters in "lag," "lamed" plus "gimel" represent thirty-three). Rabbinic tradition says that it was on this thirty-third day of the omer that the plague was lifted from the armies of Akiva for a day, so it is a time to rejoice. Orthodox Jews do not shave, cut their hair, or celebrate weddings during this time of semi-mourning. On Lag B'Omer there may be rejoicing. It is customary to give a young

Orthodox boy his first haircut on this day. Sfirat HaOmer is a rather unusual period filled with intriguing customs.

## New Testament Observance

Since it is often overshadowed by the grandeur of Passover, one wonders if Sfirat HaOmer has any significance in the New Testament. Indeed, the holiday is mentioned in the New Testament a number of times and my personal conviction is that it should be one of the most important festivals for believers in Yeshua. A close reading of I Corinthians 15 will show the vital link of Sfirat HaOmer to the ministry of Messiah. As Rabbi Saul of Tarsus teaches the believers about the doctrine of the resurrection, he makes an amazing connection to this biblical holy day:

> But the fact is that the Messiah has been raised from the dead, the firstfruits of those who have died. For since death came through a man, also the resurrection of the dead has come through a man. For just as in connection with Adam all die, so in connection with the Messiah all will be made alive. But each in his own order: the Messiah is the firstfruits; then those who belong to Messiah at the time of his coming...(I Corinthians 15:20–23).

Although many read this passage as a commentary on the order of the resurrection, Paul is actually making a technical reference to the holy day of Sfirat HaOmer. It is not merely that Yeshua was the first to rise bodily from the grave, but that by so doing, he is the direct fulfillment of the feast of First Fruits! This makes perfect sense as we reflect on the details of the day.

## The Prophetic Fulfillment

The traditional observance of this feast points us to the resurrection of Messiah. It is a harvest festival and the barley sheaves are waved before the Lord. Think of it: the grain that had come from the earth was now lifted up high for all to see! Yeshua himself alluded to his resurrection in similar terms when he said:

> The time has come for the Son of Man to be glorified. Yes, indeed!

*I tell you that unless a grain of wheat that falls to the ground dies, it stays just a grain; but if it dies, it produces a big harvest.... As for me, when I am lifted up from the earth, I will draw everyone to myself* (John 12:23–24, 32).

Coincidentally, this parable was spoken to his Jewish disciples as they had come to celebrate the Passover, just before Sfirat HaOmer (John 12:1, 20). The resurrection of Messiah from the dead is perfectly symbolized in the wave offering of the first fruits.

The connection does not stop there. Besides the rather obvious typology through the customs of Sfirat HaOmer, the actual timing of the holiday verifies this fulfillment. You will recall the controversy that developed among the early rabbis over the phrase "after the Sabbath." The Sadducees held to the seventh-day Sabbath view while the Pharisees thought Leviticus 23:11 alluded to the Sabbath of Passover. We may wonder which of the two is correct and how it relates to the resurrection of Yeshua. In a strange way that only God could arrange, both views fit the historical situation of the Gospels.

The most widely accepted traditional view says that Yeshua celebrated his last seder with his disciples on the evening of 14 Nisan, a Thursday night that particular year. He was arrested that night and stood before the Roman authorities. He was finally placed on the execution cross at 9:00 a.m. on Friday and gave up his spirit at 3:00 p.m. that afternoon, just before the weekly Sabbath. His body was quickly buried by his sympathizers, left in the tomb through that next day until, at their earliest opportunity, the women came to the tomb to find it open.

According to Jewish reckoning, therefore, Yeshua was in the tomb three days: part of Friday until sundown, sundown Friday to sundown Saturday, and day three starting at sundown Saturday. Although his empty tomb was discovered at daybreak Sunday morning, according to Jewish reckoning Yeshua could have been raised from the dead any time after sundown on Saturday. Personally, I wonder if God, our father, would not take the first possible opportunity to raise his son after Saturday sundown instead of waiting for Sunday morning!

As we trace this chronology, we can see the sovereign hand of God in regard to the timing of Sfirat HaOmer. It was imperative for Messiah to die exactly on Passover in order to fulfill the prophecies. So too Messiah must be risen from the dead on First Fruits.

At first glance there may appear to be a problem with this since there was controversy over the dating of the holy day by the first-century rabbis. But a closer look reveals that Yeshua of Nazareth fulfilled both of these interpretations in the particular year of his death and resurrection.

Yeshua was raised on the third day of Passover (16 Nisan), which fulfilled the Pharisaic interpretation of the Torah. Amazingly, he also fulfilled the Sadducean interpretation at the same time. In the particular year of his death, Sfirat HaOmer would have started on the Sunday after Passover. Consequently, the year of Yeshua's death and resurrection was one of the few in which both rabbinical theories could be correct at the same time! Indeed, God's sovereign plan should be seen by all. Blessed be he who has revealed the risen Messiah Yeshua, the fulfillment of Sfirat HaOmer!

### A PRACTICAL GUIDE FOR BELIEVERS IN MESSIAH

Having discovered the theme of Sfirat HaOmer (resurrection), believers in Messiah should appreciate the importance of the holy day. In fact, there is irony here.

The believers of the early Church, especially the Roman Church of the fourth century, began to loose touch with the Jewish understanding of the faith. However, the Church wanted to maintain a celebration of the resurrection of Messiah.

Hence, the Council of Nicea (325 C.E.) established, among other edicts, that Christians would not be allowed to commemorate Passover but would observe the resurrection on a new holiday called Easter. According to this Church, a "Western" Church, Easter would be observed on the Sunday after the Spring Equinox. Consequently, today many Christians have forgotten the intimate connection between the resurrection and the Jewish holy days.

It makes one wonder if it would have been simpler and clearer to continue to celebrate the great works of God at his appointed times. Is it any wonder that the Church historically has had such little awareness of its own Jewish heritage? In these latter days, it is wonderful to see so many believers, Jews and Gentiles, desiring to understand the original context of the faith. Sfirat HaOmer can be a beautiful celebration to point to the risen savior of the world, Yeshua HaMashiach!

In practical terms, a messianic celebration of First Fruits can celebrate the waving of the omer after sundown. Jewish tradition today is fairly simple, and consists primarily of counting the days and chanting the appropriate blessings. Messianic believers should have no problem incorporating them into their observance.

*Barukh atah Adonai Elohenu melekh ha-olam, asher kidshanu b'mitzvohtav l'hayot or l'goyeem v'natan-lanu Yeshua m'sheekhaynu ha-or la-olam.*

*Blessed art thou, O Lord Our God, King of the universe, who has sanctified us by thy commandments and commanded us to be a light unto the nations and has given us Yeshua our Messiah, the light of the world.*

*Barukh atah Adonai Elohenu melekh ha-olam, boray p'ree ha-gahfen.*

*Blessed art thou, O Lord our God, King of the universe, who creates the fruit of the vine.*

*Barukh atah Adonai Elohenu melekh ha-olam, ha-motzee lekhem meen ha-aretz.*

*Blessed art Thou, O Lord our God, King of the universe, who brings forth bread from the earth.*

You may want to say the blessings over sheaves of barley or a cup of grain, lifting them up to illustrate the truth of this holy day. An appropriate time to recount these blessings is just before the holiday dinner.

Hopefully you are within driving distance of a messianic fellowship and are able to celebrate the holy day in a larger body of believers. Although our particular group does not choose to observe Easter Sunday, we find the same message celebrated through the Jewish feast. Once it is understood, the typology of First Fruits will be appreciated by many. It points to resurrection.

In addition to the traditional blessings over the omer, other elements of a messianic First Fruits service might include worship music and a scriptural message regarding the centrality of resurrection to our faith in Yeshua. He is risen indeed!

# Sfirat Haomer Crafts

## LIVING SEED

### Materials:
plant seeds (beans are especially good)
potting soil
cups
printed bible verse sheets (John 12:24)

### Directions:
Mix soil with water in a mixing bowl. Tape or glue verse onto the cup. Fill with soil and press 2 or 3 seeds into the soil. Instruct the children to keep the soil *moist*.

# Sfirat Haomer Music

## Lion of Judah

*by Ted Sandquist*
*Used by permission*

2. Lion of Judah come to earth, I want to thank You for Your birth; for the Living Word, for Your death on the tree, for Your resurrection victory. Hallelujah! Hallelujah!
3. Lion of Judah come again, take up Your throne, Jerusalem. Bring release to this earth, and the consummation of Your kingdom's reign, let it come. Maranatha! Maranatha!
4. Repeat Verse 1

# Shavuot

## The Latter First Fruits

### THE HISTORICAL BACKGROUND

*From the day after the Sabbath, the day you brought the sheaf of the wave offering, count off seven full weeks. Count off fifty days up to the day after the seventh Sabbath, and then present an offering of new grain to the Lord. From wherever you live, bring two loaves made of two-tenths of an ephah of a fine flour, baked with yeast, as a wave offering of firstfruits to the Lord. Present with this bread seven male lambs, each a year old and without defect, one young bull and two rams. They will be a burnt offering to the Lord, together with their grain offerings and drink offerings—an offering made by fire, an aroma pleasing to the Lord. Then sacrifice one male goat for a sin offering and two lambs, each a year old, for a fellowship offering. The priest is to wave the two lambs before the Lord as a wave offering, together with the bread of the firstfruits. They are a sacred offering to the Lord for the priest. On that same day you are to proclaim a sacred assembly and do no regular work. This is to be a lasting ordinance for the generations to come, wherever you live* (Leviticus 23:15–21).

The significance of this holy day, like most other biblical festivals, can be largely understood by its name. In this passage the holy day is called *Bikkurim* (First Fruits), because it is a day of bringing first fruits as an offering to God.

From the context of the last chapter, on Sfirat Haomer, we know that this name refers to the latter fruits of the spring harvest. Previously, the early first fruits (barley) were brought in and waved before the Lord. Fifty days later, the latter first fruits (wheat) were offered to the Lord.

First Fruits is one of the *shelosh regalim*, the three festivals for which every Jewish male goes to Jerusalem if possible (Deuteronomy 16:16). First Fruits is included in this exclusive list. It is prophetically significant in God's plan for his people.

This holy day is better known by two other names. Jewish people know it as *Shavuot* (Weeks) because it occurs seven weeks after a specific event (Deuteronomy 16:10). Greek-speaking Jews and many non-Jewish Christians called this day "Pentecost" (fiftieth) because it occurs fifty days after the given day (Leviticus 23:16).

Shavuot is designated as a time of thanksgiving for the early harvest. God's faithfulness in providing the early wheat harvest increases hopefulness for an abundant fall harvest (*Sukkot*). Giving thanks for present provision leads to faith for future addition. What a wonderful God we have! He provides all our needs through his riches in glory in Messiah (Philippians 4:19)!

## TRADITIONAL JEWISH OBSERVANCE

Traditional Jewish observance of Shavuot is multi-faceted, and has evolved somewhat from biblical times. As recorded in the Torah, biblical observance centered around grain and animal offerings. Part of the wheat offering was baked into two loaves of leavened bread, a striking contrast to the matzah a few weeks before. Leaven symbolically represents sin. These two loaves were brought into the Temple and, with great ceremony, waved in every direction before the

Lord. This act was a public statement of God's provision for all his people (Mishna Bikkurim 3:2).

Another lesson of this feast relates to the presenter's need for atonement. This can be seen in the animal sacrifices that accompanied the wheat offering. The vicarious offering of the lambs, bull and rams was to symbolize the need for an innocent victim to remove sin from the people. Leviticus 17:11 summarizes the theme of the Torah sacrifices:

*For the life of a creature is in the blood, and I have given it to you to make atonement for yourselves on the altar; it is the blood that makes atonement for one's life.*

These sacrifices foreshadow the fulfillment—Yeshua, the Messiah, the perfect sacrifice for atonement!

Since the destruction of the Temple in 70 C.E., modern Jewish observance of Shavuot has changed. It is still a time to remember God's faithfulness; however, an additional, fascinating tradition has evolved. Rabbis discovered that the Israelites came to Mount Sinai in the third month after Passover (Exodus 19:1). Shavuot is the day Moses received the Law to deliver to the people. Modern observance includes celebrating the giving of the Torah. Hence, the rabbinic name for Shavuot is *Zman Matan Torateynu* (the Time of the Giving of our Law).

This conviction affects the customs of this holy day. The synagogue is usually decorated in greenery, flowers and baskets of fruit to symbolize the harvest aspect of Shavuot. The Scripture reading is Exodus 19–20 (the giving of the Law), and Ezekiel 1 (the prophet's vision of God's glory). The scroll of Ruth is also read since it takes place during the spring harvest.

Another special custom, *Tikun Leil Shavuot* (Preparing for the Arrival of Shavuot), developed from the Jewish people's love for the Torah. Traditional Jews stay up the first night of this holy day studying the Torah.

Many synagogues customarily hold confirmation services for teenagers during this season to recognize their culminated childhood studies of the Torah.

Talmudic rabbis attributed a messianic significance to Shavuot. In Tractate Sanhedrin 93b of the Talmud an interesting discussion is recorded concerning some of the details in the scroll of Ruth. Spiritual significance is ascribed to the six measures of barley Ruth presented to Boaz (Ruth 3:15). Some rabbis considered these six measures representative of six famous descendants of Ruth the Moabitess. These six include David, Daniel and King Messiah! Believers in Yeshua easily recognize the great messianic significance of the latter first fruits.

Home celebration of Shavuot follows many of the same customs of other biblical holy days. As Pentecost approaches, the holiday table is set with the best linen and dishes. The *yom tov* (holiday) candles are kindled by the woman of the house. After the traditional blessings and prayer, blessings are chanted over the cup of wine or kosher grape juice (kiddush). The challah bread is then blessed and shared by all.

A traditional holiday dinner with foods symbolizing Shavuot is then served. Milk products are appropriate because Scripture is often described as "the milk of the word" (I Peter 2:2). Cheese blintzes and cheesecake are commonly served during Shavuot. All of these customs are to remind Israel that Shavuot is a wonderful and important feast of the Lord.

## New Testament Observance

This festival is mentioned a number of times in the New Testament. Rabbi Saul of Tarsus planned his travels in correlation with Shavuot (I Corinthians 16:8). The most famous record of this holy day appears in the book of Acts:

*The festival of Shavuot arrived, and the believers all gathered together in one place. Suddenly there came a sound from the sky like the roar of a violent wind, and it filled the whole house where they were sitting. Then they saw what looked like tongues of fire, which separated and came to rest on each one of them. They were all filled with the* Ruach HaKodesh *and began to talk in different languages, as the Spirit enabled them to speak. Now there were staying in Yerushalayim religious Jews from every nation under heaven. Amazed and confused, they all went on asking each other, "What can this mean?"* (Acts 2:1–5, 12).

This account is interesting considering the background of Pentecost. To the traditional Jewish community it has always been a day of thanking God for the early harvest, trusting in a latter harvest. What was understood in the physical realm of the Torah was made manifest in the spiritual realm of New Covenant times. This has become the most famous first fruits. The early fruits have come in; the implicit promise of the latter harvest will also come.

## THE PROPHETIC FULFILLMENT

This synchronizes with promises in Scripture of latter-day messianic Jewish revival. Increasing numbers of Jewish people will believe in Yeshua until in the final day "all Israel will be saved" (Romans 11:26). I personally believe that the growing revival among Jews believing in the Messiah today indicates that we are drawing close to that time. The explosive growth of the messianic Jewish movement testifies to this modern reality.

Acts 2 reveals amazing details confirming the Jewish background of this New Testament Pentecost. Ezekiel 1 is the tradi-tional reading from the prophets for Shavuot. This passage dramatically describes Ezekiel's vision of the glory of God. He describes the tremendous manifestation in these terms:

*I looked, and I saw a windstorm coming out of the north—an immense cloud with flashing lightning and surrounded by brilliant light. The center of the fire looked like glowing metal* (Ezekiel 1:4).

Imagine thousands of Jewish worshipers leaving the Temple after the morning service (at the third hour, Acts 2:15) having just read the passage from Ezekiel 1. Suddenly some of the same manifestations of the Holy Spirit started to appear before their eyes! No wonder they were amazed and perplexed by the windstorm and fire. It certainly got their attention! They must have wondered if God was revealing his *Shekinah* glory for the first time in nearly 600 years! The glory of God was present at the giving of the Law; the same glory was manifested at the giving of the holy spirit. The prophet later wrote: "I will put my Spirit in you and cause you to walk in my statutes..." (Ezekiel 36:27).

These Jewish pilgrims, who had come from all over the dispersion, were hearing the impossible. These Galilean disciples were speaking various languages with such an exact "dialect" that the crowds saw it as an irrefutable miracle. Having received their undivided attention through these acts of God, Peter was able to preach a powerful sermon about Messiah Yeshua, and 3000 Jews responded to salvation. The first fruits of believers had come in a wonder-full way!

The apostle James, in his letter to the Jewish believers (James 1:1), emphasizes this historical fact as he reminds his readers:

> *Having made his decision, he gave birth to us through a word that can be relied upon, in order that we should be a kind of firstfruits of all that he created* (James 1:18).

The theme of Shavuot can be best summed up by the word revival. Israel was called to praise God for the first fruits of the ground, knowing that these early fruits assured the latter harvest. This also applies to the spiritual Kingdom of God. The first fruits of believers at Shavuot virtually guarantees a revival in the latter-day spiritual harvest for Messiah. Now we can understand why God included Shavuot in the three required festivals for every Jewish male. As Passover speaks of redemption, Shavuot speaks of revival, especially during this era. The message of Shavuot is one of great hope and joy. May the day come soon when the holy spirit will be poured out upon the house of David, and they will all look, in faith, to the one who was pierced (Zechariah 12:10).

## A Practical Guide for Believers in Messiah

With all the spiritual meaning behind the holy day of Shavuot, believers in Yeshua can find great blessing in celebrating it. Much of the traditional Jewish observance can be followed. Yet, as believers add messianic perspective to this feast, it becomes more meaningful.

The practical celebration of Shavuot begins when Sfirat Haomer ends. On the day before the start of Pentecost, a number of preparations should be made for the observance. The dinner table is set with the best linens and dishes. You may want to decorate the house with greenery or fresh flowers, a reminder of the harvest aspect of the day. As the sun is setting on Erev Shavuot (evening of Pentecost), the family and friends gather around the festive table. The holiday candles are lit and the following blessings are recited:

*Barukh atah Adonai Elohenu melekh ha-olam, asher kidshanu b'mitzvohtav l'hayot or l'goyeem v'natan-lanu Yeshua m'shee-khaynu ha-or la-olam.*

*Blessed art thou, O Lord our God, King of the universe, who has sanctified us by thy commandments and commanded us to be a light unto the nations and has given us Yeshua, our Messiah, the Light of the World.*

On the first night of the holy day we add:

*Barukh atah Adonai Elohenu melekh ha-olam, she-he-khiyanu v'kiya-manu v'higi-yanu lazman hazeh.*

*Blessed are thou, O Lord our God, King of the universe, who has given us life, sustained us and brought us to this season.*

The blessings over the wine and challah are chanted to traditional melodies. Next, the holiday dinner is served, which should include dairy dishes to help commemorate the milk, that is the Word of God. God's Word becomes a special joy to believers in Yeshua because his holy spirit enables believers to follow his instructions.

Many messianic congregations hold Erev Shavuot services and morning services the next day. Corporate worship and fellowship are consistent with the intent of Pentecost. After the evening service, some ambitious believers might want to have their own Tikun Leil Shavuot (preparing for the night of pentecost). As we learned earlier, this is the tradition of staying up late to study Torah. A messianic group of believers might focus on the five books of Moses and the blessings of the holy spirit. Whatever customs are incorporated, the holy day of Shavuot can be a true blessing for those who have the holy spirit within them.

# Recipes for Shavuot

## BLINTZES

**Ingredients:**

*Crepes:*
1 cup flour
1/2 teaspoon salt
4 eggs
1 cup milk
Butter or magarine to fry with

*Filling:*
1 cup dry cottage cheese
1/2 cup sour cream
2 tablespoons sugar
1 teaspoon vanilla

**Directions:**

Mix crepe ingredients. Butter and heat a skillet. Pour about 1/2 cup of batter onto the pan, forming a large circle. Cook on one side only, until the blintz starts to "blister" and the edges curl away from the skillet. Ease onto a board fried-side up. Continue cooking until the rest of the batter is used up, adding margarine to the skillet as needed.

Mix filling ingredients. Place about 2 tablespoons of filling onto the cooked-side of each crepe. Fold the top and bottom to the center. Roll the sides over. Return to pan and fry lightly until the center is cooked.

## NOODLE KUGEL

•Note: Mix ingredients and refrigerate overnight before baking.

**Ingredients:**

1 lb. medium noodles
2 pints sour cream
3 cups half-and-half cream
7 eggs
1 1/2 cup sugar
4 oz. melted margarine
1 teaspoon vanilla

1 cup white raisins
1/2 cup cornflake crumbs
1 teaspoon cinnamon
2 teaspoons sugar

**Directions:**
Boil noodles until done. Drain. In a large bowl, mix well the sourcream, cream, eggs, sugar, margarine and vanilla. Add the noodles and raisins. Pour into a large greased pan at least 10x15 inches. Mix cornflake crumbs, cinnamon and sugar. Cover the casserole. Cover with foil and refrigerate before baking. Turn oven on to 350°; bake for 1 1/2 hours.

## MINIATURE CHEESECAKES

**Ingredients:**
12 vanilla wafers
2, 8 oz. packages cream cheese
1/2 cup sugar
1 teaspoon vanilla
2 eggs

**Directions:**
Line cupcake pan with foil liners. Place one vanilla wafer in each liner. Mix cream cheese, vanilla and sugar on medium speed until well blended. Add eggs and mix well. Pour over wafers, filling 3/4 full and bake at 325° for 25 minutes. Remove from pan when cool. Chill and top with fruit, preserves, nuts, chocolate or pie filling.

# Shavuot Crafts

### THE TEN COMMANDMENTS GIVEN AT SINAI

**Materials:**
cups
paper
pens
tablet design

**Directions:**
Cut paper rectangles that will fit over an upside down cup. Have students decorate this to look like a mountain with rocks, plants, and grass. Tape or staple onto a cup. Cut out the tablet design and glue or staple on the top. Write "Mt. Sinai" and "Exodus 20" on the cups.

### HOLY SPIRIT HEADBAND

**Materials:**
construction paper

**Directions:**
Cut long strips of construction paper that will fit around a child's head. Draw flames on pieces of paper and have child cut out. Attach flames to band with glue, tape, or staples. Write "Tongues of fire filled with the holy spirit, Acts 2." Then size the band on the child's head before stapling band into a circle.

# A Word about the Interlude Between the Holy Days

With the close of Shavuot, we come to an ending to the spring holy day season. It started with the redemption of Pesach, followed by the resurrection of Sfirat Haomer and culminated by the revival of First Fruits. Historically these three holy days have already been fulfilled according to God's calendar of events. Accordingly, there is now a gap of time during the long summer in which there are no biblical holy days. The crops will grow during the summer months until the arrival of the fall holidays that speak of events just prior to the second coming of Messiah. As Yeshua himself said:

> "Now let the fig tree teach you its lesson: when its branches begin to sprout and leaves appear, you know that summer is approaching. In the same way, when you see all these things, you are to know that the time is near, right at the door" (Matthew 24:32–33).

We are presently in that long, hot summer in which God is growing what will be harvested . Many signs indicate that the summer is quickly drawing to a close and the fulfillment of the fall holidays is about to begin. Are we ready for the return of Messiah? Are we working to help bring in the harvest of these latter days?

# **5**

# **⌇Rosh HaShanah**

The New Year

## THE HISTORICAL BACKGROUND

*The Lord said to Moses, "Say to the Israelites: 'On the first day of the seventh month you are to have a day of rest, a sacred assembly commemorated with trumpet blasts. Do no regular work, but present an offering made to the Lord by fire'"* (Leviticus 23:23–25).

One of the fascinating facts about the holy day, *Rosh HaShanah* is that it is considered the "New Year." The truth is, it comes in the seventh month of the calendar year. Did someone make a blatant miscalculation?

The biblical year starts in the spring with the month Nisan (Exodus 12:2). This has a certain logic to it. It is the beginning of the new harvest season.

However, the rabbis gave such significance to this special Shabbat (it was the first of the fall holidays) that they eventually considered it as the "spiritual" New Year. Hence the name change as well. Biblically known as *Yom Teruah* (the Day of Sounding/Festival of Trumpets), this first day of Tishri became called "Rosh HaShanah," the Head of the Year.

The purpose of this holy day is summed up in one word—regathering. Since the fall holidays call us to regather to a pure faith in God, Rosh HaShanah has come to represent the day of repentance. It is the day when the people of Israel take stock of their spiritual condition and make the necessary changes to insure that the upcoming new year will be pleasing to God.

So important is this day of Rosh HaShanah that, in fact, the entire preceding Hebrew month of Elul takes on a holy significance of its own. The rabbis stressed that the forty day period from the first day of Elul through the tenth day of Tishri (Yom Kippur) was to be a time of special spiritual preparation. This was based on the belief that it was on the first of Elul that Moses ascended Mount Sinai in order to receive the second set of Tablets of the Law and that he descended on Yom Kippur (*Pirke DeRabbi Eliezer* 46).

## TRADITIONAL JEWISH OBSERVANCE

In synagogues the *shofar*, or ram's horn, is sounded daily to alert the faithful that the time of repentance is near. Many Orthodox men take a special water immersion (Hebrew, *tevilah mikveh*) to symbolize cleansing their ways.

Since the theme of Rosh HaShanah is repentance, the observance takes on a somber character, yet always with a hint of hope because of God's forgiveness. In the traditional Jewish home, the evening starts with the festival dinner with many of the customary dishes. Then it is off to synagogue for the evening service. A good part of the next day is also spent in worship.

The liturgy, music and prayers emphasize the recurring theme of repentance, turning to God. Since the day is a shabbat, most Jewish people take off from work or school in order to observe the day correctly.

In traditional groups, the afternoon of Rosh HaShanah is spent at a body of water (ocean, lake or stream) observing the ancient service, *Tashlich*. The word derives from Micah 7:19 where the prophet promises, "You will hurl all our iniquities into the depths of the sea." To illustrate this beautiful truth, people cast bread crumbs or pebbles into the water and rejoice in God's promise of forgiveness.

With these themes in mind, it is customary in the Jewish community to send holiday cards greeting family and friends with wishes for a blessed New Year.

The most noticeable custom is the *shofar*, the trumpet mentioned in the biblical text. The shofar is sounded in the synagogue with four different notes: *tekia* (blast), *shevarim* (broken notes), *teruah* (alarm) and *tekia gedolah* (the great blast). These notes provide some spiritual lessons. Rabbis observed that the shofar was used in the ancient world to hail a king. So, too, at Rosh HaShanah, all Israel is said to appear before the King of Kings in anticipation of personal judgement. Also, often in the Bible the shofar was sounded to gather the troops together for battle (see Joshua 6). In this case, the shofar is our "wake-up call"; an alarm to call us to our appointed time.

## THE PROPHETIC FULFILLMENT

As with all biblical holy days, there is prophetic as well as historical meaning in Rosh HaShanah. Many classical rabbis saw a connection between Rosh HaShanah as the holy day of regathering and the Messiah who would be the agent of regathering. For example, in a work in the 8th century C.E. we find the following commentary:

> *Messiah ben David (son of David), Elijah and Zerubbabel, peace be upon him, will ascend the Mount of Olives. And Messiah will command Elijah to blow the shofar. The light of the six days of*

*Creation will return and will be seen, the light of the moon will be like the light of the sun, and God will send full healing to all the sick of Israel. The second blast which Elijah will blow will make the dead rise. They will rise from the dust and each man will recognize his fellow man, and so will husband and wife, father and son, brother and brother. All will come to the Messiah from the four corners of the earth, from east and from west, from north and from south. The Children of Israel will fly on the wings of eagles and come to the Messiah...* (Ma'ase Daniel as quoted in Patai, p.143).

While the historical emphasis of the holy day is repentance, the prophetic theme looks for the future day when the full spiritual regathering will occur under the Messiah.

All the details of Rosh HaShanah become more interesting as we consider the New Testament and the life of Yeshua. The bulk of biblical evidence has led me to agree with those who say the Messiah's birth took place in the late fall, not the winter (see chapter on "Sukkot"). If this is true, we can approximate the time when Yeshua started his public ministry. As Luke notes in his Gospel (3:23), Yeshua was "about thirty years old" thus placing his baptism and first preaching in the fall of that year.

Consider the parallel themes to Rosh HaShanah. Would it be surprising that Yeshua took a special immersion/mikveh in the fall of the year (Matthew 3:13–17)? Is there a relationship to the forty day period of testing by the adversary (Matthew 4:1–11)? And what was the message Yeshua immediately started proclaiming after the forty days? "Turn from your sins to God, for the Kingdom of Heaven is near!"

What better time could there have been for the Messiah to start his earthly ministry than the time of the spiritual new year? The historical evidence seems to indicate the month of Elul served as the perfect time of preparation for the greatest spiritual message ever to come to Israel: return to God, Messiah has come!

There is rich prophetic truth associated with this Feast of Trumpets. As it characterizes a time of ingathering and spiritual preparation, a future fulfillment of Rosh HaShanah is also alluded to. In speaking of the future regathering of the believers in Messiah, commonly called the "Rapture," Rabbi Saul (the apostle Paul) reveals an interesting connection to the holy day:

> For the Lord himself will come down from heaven with a rousing cry, with a call from one of the ruling angels, and with God's shofar; those who died united with the Messiah will be the first to rise; then we who are left still alive will be caught up (Latin = rapture) with them in the clouds to meet the Lord in the air; and thus we will always be with the Lord. So encourage each other with these words" (I Thessalonians 4:16–18).

This holy day is a perfect picture of the regathering of believers! In the future all true believers in Yeshua will be gathered to meet him in the clouds. The dead in Messiah will rise first, to be followed immediately by those believers alive at that time. Not surprisingly, the signal of the gathering will be the sound of the shofar. In fact, the reference here is to a particular note sounded at Rosh HaShanah. The word normally translated "shout" in verse sixteen comes from the Hebrew, teruah, better translated in this context as the "alarm" blast of the shofar. Similar references to the shofar as the signal of the Rapture can be found elsewhere in the New Testament (see I Corinthians 15:50–58 and Revelation 4:1).

Another important fulfillment of Rosh HaShanah is the regathering of the Jewish believing remnant at the second coming of Messiah. As far back as the seventh century B.C.E., the prophet Isaiah wrote:

> In that day the Lord will thresh from the flowing Euphrates to the Wadi of Egypt, and you, O Israelites will be gathered up one by one. And in that day a great trumpet will sound. Those who were perishing in Assyria and those who were exiled in Egypt will come and worship the Lord on the holy mountain in Jerusalem" (Isaiah 27:12–13).

That this passage is referring to a latter day regathering of the believing remnant is clear, and we are still waiting for this shofar to fulfill it. Likewise, Messiah Yeshua, when asked about the future of Israel, confirmed this as a latter day promise in his own teaching:

*He (the Son of Man) will send out his angels with a great shofar; and they will gather together his chosen people from the four winds, from one end of heaven to the other"* (Matthew 24:31).

Believers in Yeshua HaMashiach should have a fond appreciation for this rich holy day, Rosh HaShanah! It has served historically as a time of spiritual preparation and repentance, both themes we can learn from. Prophetically, we are reminded of God's promise to regather and restore his chosen people, Israel, in the last day. The sound of the shofar is also a reminder of the blessed hope every messianic believer possesses: we could enter Messiah's presence at any time (Titus 2:13). Let us give heed to the sound of the shofar and all that Rosh HaShanah has to teach.

**A PRACTICAL GUIDE FOR BELIEVERS IN MESSIAH**

There are a number of practical ways to observe Rosh HaShanah. In synagogues, preparation starts the preceding Hebrew month, Elul, by sounding the shofar on Shabbat. Special prayers to cultivate repentance, called *selikhot*, are offered. For Messianic Jews and Gentiles this season could be observed in the same kind of spirit. Perhaps one might desire to purchase a shofar and sound it every morning during the month preceding Rosh HaShanah. This could be used to enhance the true spirit of this holy day—focusing on repentance and a pure walk with God.

A special evening observance can be planned upon reaching the first day of Tishri. As with most Jewish holy days, much of the preparation revolves around a holiday meal. The table is set with the best dinnerware, tablecloth and two candlesticks. White is a common color for the holy days based on the promise that God will turn our scarlet sins as white as snow (Isaiah 1:18). This may include the tablecloth, and often, personal clothing. To believers it is a beautiful statement of our cleansing in Yeshua! It is traditional to light the holiday candles with the appropriate blessing which is slightly different from the standard Shabbat blessing.

*Barukh atah Adonai Elohenu melekh ha-olam, asher kidshanu b'mitzvohtav, v'tzi-vanu l'hadleek ner shel yom tov.*

*Blessed art thou, O Lord Our God, King of the universe, who has set us apart by your commandments and has commanded us to kindle the holiday light.*

After the candles, we bless the sweet wine and the special round raisin challah bread. Both remind us of an important theme of Rosh HaShanah—that we will experience a sweet and full New Year in God's blessing.

The foods of the dinner also make this statement. We may have the traditional *tzimmes* (carrots with honey), as well as honey cake for dessert. In one of the more graphic customs, we dip sliced apples in honey to taste the incredible sweetness that comes from our heavenly father. It should be noted that the traditional greeting of the holiday season is *l'shana tova u-metukah* (may you have a sweet and good new year). Main dishes might be turkey or brisket. A symbolic dish is a cooked fish served with its head. This illustrates God's promise that there will be a time when Israel will no longer be the tail, but the head (Deuteronomy 28:13)!

After the dinner it is time to celebrate in worship and in meditation. Normally, this takes place in the synagogue service. The purchase of tickets ahead of time is usually necessary since Jews do not ordinarily pass a plate at services. Membership fees and individual tickets for the high holy days are charged.

Believers in Yeshua might attend Rosh HaShanah services at a local messianic congregation. Here you will celebrate the various customs of the holy day among fellow believers. What a joy to hear the sound of the shofar, to experience the corporate prayers, and to worship in music in the fulness of Messiah! If there is no messianic group nearby, perhaps a home service is in order. This could include many of the same elements to draw attention to this special day.

Since this is a shabbat, the following day can be made special by taking off from normal work and school. Usually, there is a special service on the morning of Rosh HaShanah to continue in corporate worship of the King. After the morning services, customarily in late afternoon, the special ceremony called Tashlikh is held. What a meaningful service this can be for believers—to cast bread crumbs, symbolizing sins, into a body of water! The shofar can be sounded, and a guitar played while songs of praise are sung to celebrate the truth of Micah 7:19!

Being in a warmer climate, our San Diego group has even had a group immersion service at this time, culminated in a fellowship picnic. Whether at home or in a congregational setting, Rosh HaShanah can be a wonderful time of spiritual revival, preparing to be gathered to the King of Kings, Yeshua!

# Rosh HaShanah Recipes

## HONEYCAKE

**Ingredients:**
- 1/2 cup oil
- 1/3 cup honey
- 1/3 cup packed brown sugar
- 1 cup applesauce
- 1 1/2 cups flour
- 1 1/4 cups teaspoons baking soda
- 1/4 teaspoon salt
- 1 teaspoon cinnamon
- 1/2 teaspoon nutmeg, optional
- 1/4 teaspoon ground cloves, optional

**Directions:**
Mix oil, honey, sugar and applesauce. Add dry ingredients, mixing thoroughly. Pour into greased 8 or 9 inch square pan. Recipe can be doubled and place in a 9x13 inch pan. Bake at 350° for 35-40 minutes.

## SOLE ROLL-UPS

**Ingredients:**
- 1 medium size onion
- 1 tablespoon oil
- 4 small sole fillets (about 6 oz. each)
- 1 medium size zucchini (about 10 oz.)
- 1 14-1/2–16 ounce can stewed tomatoes
- 1/2 teaspoon dried basil leaves
- 1/8 teaspoon pepper

**Directions:**
Chop onion, cook in oil in a 10 inch skillet until tender (about 5 minutes). Sprinkle one side of fillets with salt. Roll each fillet, salt-side in, starting with a short end. Cut zucchini into 1/2 inch chunks. Add stewed tomatoes, basil, pepper and 1 teaspoon salt, stirring to break up tomatoes. Add zucchini. Place sole roll-ups in tomato mixture, seamside down. Turn up heat until mixture boils, then reduce heat, cover and simmer for 15 minutes or until sole flakes easily.

## Tzimmes

**Ingredients:**
2 lbs. carrots, peeled and sliced
1/4 cup orange juice concentrate
1/2 cup honey
2 lbs canned yams, drained
1 lb. pineapple chunks
3/4 lb. dried fruit mix, chopped
1/2 cup raisins
1 tablespoon pumpkin pie spice.

**Directions:**
Steam carrots until soft. Mix with remaining ingredients in a large saucepan. Cook over low heat until fruit is soft and everything is heated through.

# Rosh HaShanah Crafts

## SHOFAR

### Materials:
Heavy grade paper (tag board)
tape
pens

### Directions:
Color and decorate paper; roll the paper into a cone; tape. Wet your lips and blow in same manner as a kazoo.

## BIRTHDAY CAKE FOR CREATION

### Materials:
Cake mix
cake ingredients
bowl
pan
oven
decorator frosting.

### Directions:
Mix and bake a cake according to package directions. After frosting, write "Happy Birthday World" with decorator frosting.

## JERUSALEM PICTURE

### Materials:
Large construction paper for background
glue
pens
cut outs of Jerusalem-style buildings
greenery.
Rosh Hashana cards with Jerusalem pictures—optional

### Directions:
Student may either cut their own designs or use pre-cut designs. Glue onto background. The picture reminds us to pray for the peace of Jerusalem. It also reminds us that the coming judgement will start from Jerusalem.

## HOLY SPIRIT PICTURE

### Materials:
picture below copied onto paper
pens
mat board—optional

### Directions:
Color and glue onto a board.

Used by permission
House of David
White Stone, Virginia

# Rosh HaShanah Music

## Melech Ozair

*Adapted by Stuart Dauermann*
*Used by permission*

*Liturgy*

2. King, Redeemer, Savior and Shield; King, Redeemer, Savior and Shield.
   Blessed art Thou, O Lord, Blessed art Thou, O Lord, Shield of Abraham.
   Blessed art Thou, O Lord, Blessed art Thou, O Lord, Shield of Abraham.

3. Atah Gibbor Le'Olam va-ed; Atah Gibbor Le'Olam va-ed.
   Mechayey Meytim Atah, Mechayeh Meytim Atah, Rav LeHosiah.
   Mechayey Meytim Atah, Mechayeh Meytim Atah, Rav LeHosiah.

4. You are the Mighty One, forever O Lord; You are the Mighty One,
   forever O Lord.
   You raise the dead, sleeping in their graves, You are mighty to save.
   You raise the dead, sleeping in their graves, You are mighty to save.

# Avinu Malkeynu

Liturgy

Sing in English: (translation)

Our Father and our King
Our Father and our King
Our Father and King
Be merciful to us
Be merciful unto us.

For we have done no deeds
Commending us unto You
For we have no deeds commending us to You
Be merciful, save us, we pray.

# 6

# ![Yom Kippur](lamb icon) Yom Kippur
## The Day of Atonement

### THE HISTORICAL BACKGROUND

> The Lord said to Moses, "The tenth day of this seventh month is
> the Day of Atonement. Hold a sacred assembly and deny
> yourselves, and present an offering made to the Lord by fire. Do
> no work on that day, because it is the Day of Atonement, when
> atonement is made for you before the Lord your God. Anyone
> who does not deny himself on that day must be cut off from his
> people. I will destroy from among his people anyone who does any
> work on that day. You shall do no work at all. This is to be a
> lasting ordinance for the generations to come, wherever you live.
> It is a Sabbath of rest for you, and you must deny yourselves.
> From the evening of the ninth day of the month until the following
> evening you are to observe your Sabbath" (Leviticus 23:26–32).

Yom Kippur has long been considered the most holy day
in the Jewish biblical calendar. The name itself describes the

history of the holy day for it was on this very day, once a year, that the High Priest would enter the Holy of Holies to make atonement for the nation. In a word, Yom Kippur illustrates regeneration for those who follow God's way of atonement.

Leviticus 16 goes into great detail about the ceremony, centered on the sacrifices of two goats. One goat, called *Chatat* was to be slain as a blood sacrifice to symbolically cover the sins of Israel. The other goat, called *Azazel*, or Scapegoat, would be brought before the priest. The priest would lay his hands on the head of the goat as he confessed the sins of the people. But instead of slaying this animal in the traditional fashion, the goat would be set free in the wilderness symbolically taking the sins of the nation out from their midst.

What a picture this must have been of God's gracious provision. Atonement and forgiveness by way of vicarious sacrifice! This theme of Yom Kippur made it the preeminent holy day in ancient Israel. Likewise, because of its proximity to Rosh HaShanah ten days earlier, Yom Kippur's theme was all the more important. What was started on the first of Tishri, namely, repentance and self-evaluation, was completed on the tenth of the month with atonement and regeneration. There is no more important theme in the Holy Scriptures than receiving atonement for sins in God's prescribed manner!

Throughout the Temple period to today, Yom Kippur has maintained a special relationship to the Jewish people. In Temple times, the observance of the Day was more clearly defined. It centered on the sacrifices. In 70 C.E., however, the Temple was destroyed; hence, rabbis and theologians have been confronted with some perplexing questions.

How do we celebrate Yom Kippur without the proper place of sacrifice? How do we have Yom Kippur without the proper *Kaparah* sacrifice? The rabbis of the first century decided to make substitutions to fill the gap. *Tefilah* (prayer), *Teshuvah* (repentance) and *Tzedakah* (charity) replace sacrifices in the modern observance of Yom Kippur. This explains why the modern observance is so different than it was in biblical times.

There are Orthodox Jewish sects who still see the need for a Temple and animal sacrifices to be revived in Israel. The "Temple Mount Faithful" are actively reproducing the holy vessels and priestly garments to prepare for the coming Temple. They have attempted to place the first cornerstone on the Temple Mount in Jerusalem, strongly believing that such a structure will be rebuilt soon!

While the vast majority of Jews see these things as an aberration, it nonetheless points out the need for atonement as spoken of in the Bible. If one looks *carefully* at the modern synagogue observance of Yom Kippur, it will not be hard to see that the theme is still there, although submerged by tradition.

## THE TRADITIONAL JEWISH OBSERVANCE

As mentioned above, Yom Kippur is considered the logical extension of what was started at Rosh HaShanah. In fact, the ten days between Rosh HaShanah and Yom Kippur take on their own holy significance. They're called the *Yomim Nora'im*, The Days of Awe. Traditional Jews, as well as many non-traditional Jews, spend these days looking inward, seeing how their inner life might be more pleasing to God. Personal relationships are evaluated; forgiveness and restitution are offered where needed. Reconciliation is attempted.

As the evening of the 10th of Tishri approaches, special preparations are made. Leviticus 23 states that on Yom Kippur, Israel is to "humble your soul." This is taken (based on the Hebrew word *oni*) to mean "fast". In the context of Isaiah 58:5, this word is used specifically for going without food.

## A NOTE ABOUT FASTING

While I personally believe that Yom Kippur is the only biblically mandated fast, it would be good to note other days that rabbinic Judaism has considered to be fast days. The Fast of *Tisha B'Av* (9th of Av, usually in August) is observed by religious Jews to mourn the numerous tragedies that struck on that day. Among the sad events remembered are the destruction of both the first and second Temples in Jerusalem, in 586 B.C.E. and 70 C.E., respectively, and the expulsion of the Jews from Spain on this day in 1492. This is a total fast like Yom Kippur, with the scroll of Lamentations read to recall the tragic history.

The 10th of *Tevet* (around early December), which marks the beginning of the siege against Jerusalem in 586 B.C.E., is another minor fast day. The Fast of Esther (usually February or March) recalls the days of fasting and prayer before the deliverance recalled at Purim (see Chapter 9). The 17th of *Tammuz* (July) commemorates the breach of the walls of Jerusalem in 586 B.C.E. The Fast of Gedaliah (3rd of Tishri, usually September) points to the assassination of this last king of the first Temple period.

While there is no direct commandment to observe these fast days, they are mentioned in Scripture. For messianic believers in Yeshua, perhaps the most significant verse is in Zechariah. He foresees a time when these days of mourning will all be forgotten in the days of Messiah. As it is written:

*This is what the Lord Almighty says: "The fasts of the fourth, fifth, seventh and tenth months will become joyful and glad occasions and happy festivals for Judah. Therefore love truth and peace"* (Zechariah 8:19).

Won't it be wonderful when these days of mourning are finally turned to joy in the presence of Yeshua HaMashiach!

Nonetheless, Yom Kippur stands alone as a biblical fast day. Before sundown, when the fast begins, it is customary to have a holiday meal. In fact, it is a requirement in order to make the fast day set apart! As with the other holy days, the table is set with the best linens and dishes. White is still an appropriate color for linens and clothing. It symbolizes the hope of the high holy days, the cleansing from our sins (see Isaiah 1:18). The two candles are lit and the blessings are said over the wine and the challah bread.

After the festive meal, just before dark, Yom Kippur

commences along with the fast. The fast continues from sundown on the ninth of Tishri until sundown on the tenth. And, mind you, when Jews fast, we take it seriously! No food, not even water. Jews are encouraged to abstain from all luxuries for those twenty-four hours. No unnecessary bathing, entertainment, etc. Please note that the rabbis are quick to point out that the fast is only applicable to healthy adults past bar mitzvah age (thirteen). Anyone with a health problem or who is pregnant or nursing is exempted from the fast.

The evening of the holy day (Erev Yom Kippur) is perhaps the most holy occasion of the spiritual year. Jews flock to the local synagogues to attend Kol Nidre service. Kol Nidre is a special cantorial prayer asking God for release from any vows that have been taken inappropriately. The origin of the petition dates back to the Middle Ages when many Jews were forcibly converted into the church, yet still wanted to maintain their connection with their people. The evening service continues with traditional prayers and songs from the Jewish prayer book calling Israel to atonement in God.

Yom Kippur day takes on the feel of a most holy Shabbat. Jewish worshipers continue the fast that started the previous evening and likewise attend synagogue services all day. The traditional liturgy, prayers and music emphasize the theme of the day, the need for atonement for sins. The services last most of the day for it is believed that judgment will come at the close of Yom Kippur. The prayers fervently request that, as Jews, we be written in the Book of Life for one more year.

The holy day closes with an important Neilah service (the closing of the gates). The final blast of the shofar is sounded. It is thought that the fate of each individual is sealed at that time for the upcoming year. Naturally, the hope is for a sweet and blessed spiritual year, which is illustrated in the break-the-fast meal which follows sundown. Tasted first is the sweet wine, which is blessed in the traditional manner. Next, the sweet challah or honeycake is eaten as a reminder of the sweet new year that we hope to experience. For most Jews, this is at best an optimistic hope that sins have been atoned for. Believers in Yeshua can rejoice in the confidence that he, the Messiah, has indeed paid the price that God required.

## YOM KIPPUR IN THE NEW TESTAMENT

This holy day, Yom Kippur, contains important truth for the believer in Yeshua. In fact, if any holy day deserves special recognition by believers, Yom Kippur should be at the top of the list! Not surprisingly, there are a number of references to the importance of this holy day in the New Testament. In the well-known passage in Romans, Rabbi Saul of Tarsus explains the significance of our atonement in the context of Yom Kippur.

> *All have sinned and come short of earning God's praise. By God's grace, without earning it, all are granted the status of being considered righteous before him, through the act redeeming us from our enslavement to sin that was accomplished by the Messiah Yeshua. God put Yeshua forward as the kapparah for sin through his faithfulness in respect to his bloody sacrificial death. This vindicated God's righteousness; because, in his forbearance, he had passed over [with neither punishment nor remission,] the sins people had committed in the past; and it vindicates his righteousness in the present age by showing that he is righteous himself and is also the one who makes people righteous on the ground of Yeshua's faithfulness* (Romans 3:23–26).

The word translated "kapparah" (propitiation) is somewhat misunderstood today since it is not commonly used. The Greek word contains the idea of appeasing an angry Greek god. While there may be some relationship, the Hebrew equivalent of the word is clear. Kapparah means more than appeasement. It also means "atonement," a term any Jew of the first century could relate to. On the cross, Messiah Yeshua was displayed as our kapparah, our sacrifice, the fulfillment of what Yom Kippur is all about!

Since the theme of atonement is so central to the message of the New Testament, it should not be surprising to discover other references to Yom Kippur within its pages. Towards the end of the book of Acts, Rabbi Saul of Tarsus is on the final leg of his famous voyage to Rome in order to appeal the political charges against him. While speaking of the dangerous weather that had developed, the writer makes a reference stating that "it was already past Yom Kippur" (Acts 27:9). This corresponds to the inclement sailing conditions since this would have taken place in the late fall of the year.

In Luke 4:16-22, Yeshua is called to the Torah in his local synagogue of Nazareth. After reading the powerful passage from Isaiah 61, he delivered a simple yet stunning message, claiming to be the Messiah, the anointed one, who would set the captives free. Some of the classical rabbis believed this passage would be the very words Messiah would speak to Israel when he came (*Lexicon*, Rabbi David Kimchi, as quoted in A *Manual of Christian Evidences For Jewish People*, Vol. 2, p.76). The fact that this passage speaks of the Messiah as the liberator of the Jewish people led other rabbis to speculate that Messiah would appear on a very special Yom Kippur in the Year of Jubilee (see Leviticus 25:10).

*The World will endure not less than 85 Jubilees, and in the last jubilee the Messiah, Son of David, will come* (Talmud Sanhedrin 97b).

Another interesting element is that this passage of Isaiah 61 is no longer read in the traditional one-year cycle of readings in the synagogue. Yet it is known that the first-century service was based on a three-year cycle which was much more expanded. Hence, Isaiah 61 might logically have been tied to a reading close in proximity, namely Isaiah 58. Coincidently, Isaiah 58 is the current synagogue reading for every Yom Kippur service! Such information has led some scholars to conclude not only that Yeshua was presenting a dramatic message about his Messiahship, but that this event actually took place at a Yom Kippur service. (Edersheim mentions this view by Bengel in *Life and Times of Jesus the Messiah*, Book III, p. 452). Not a bad time for Yeshua to publicly speak the words that Messiah was to speak to Israel!

## THE PROPHETIC FULFILLMENT

We have seen that the theme of Yom Kippur can be clearly understood in its name, the Day of Atonement. The atonement was typologically foretold in the sacrifices and service of the holy day. Yom Kippur in the New Testament takes on special significance as we see Yeshua presented as Messiah and paying the price on the cross. Yet Yom Kippur, as the other holy days, is not to be limited to a historical lesson. It has a prophetic truth to teach all believers in Yeshua.

The prophet Zechariah spoke of a future day of repentance when God will pour out his spirit in the latter days and they will look to the one who is pierced (Zechariah 12:10). This fits the description of Rosh HaShanah in the prophetic sense, a time of repentance. What follows in chapter 13 is quite relevant. Zechariah says:

*On that day a fountain will be opened to the house of David and the inhabitants of Jerusalem, to cleanse them from sin and impurity* (Zechariah 13:1).

After Rosh HaShanah comes Yom Kippur. After repentance comes regeneration. Such is the promise for all Israel as she will supernaturally experience the fulfillment of Yom Kippur and the return of Messiah Yeshua. This corroborates the word given to Rabbi Saul:

*For brothers, I want you to understand this truth which God formerly concealed but has now revealed, so that you won't imagine you know more than you actually do. It is that stoniness, to a degree, has come upon Israel, until the Gentile world enters in its fullness; and that it is in this way that all Israel will be saved. As the Tanakh says, "Out of Tsiyon will come the Redeemer; he will turn away ungodliness from Ya'akov and this will be my covenant with them...when I take away their sins"* (Romans 11:25–27).

This is the prophetic fulfillment of Yom Kippur, the final atonement realized and received by that generation of Jews living at the second coming of Yeshua. For believers in this soon-coming King, what a picture Yom Kippur is. We can rejoice in atonement now, yet pray for the realization of this blessed hope to come to Israel soon!

## A PRACTICAL GUIDE FOR BELIEVERS IN MESSIAH

For believers in Yeshua, both Jewish and non-Jewish, the observance of Yom Kippur can hold special significance. The repentance started at Rosh HaShanah comes to a culmination with atonement ten days later. As with the traditional Jewish community, those ten days (Yomim Nora'im) can take on spiritual meaning as we meditate on the meaning of the high holy days. Although there are not many customs directly relating to the ten days, the message could be applied to a believer's daily meditation at that time. Traditional readings from the book of Jonah, Hosea 14 and other pertinent passages can enhance one's appreciation of the season.

With Erev Yom Kippur approaching late in the afternoon on the 9th of Tishri, special arrangements are made to usher in the holiest day of the year. Since it is called a Shabbat, the general customs for the Sabbath are in order. Yom Kippur will be a fast day for most, so the late-afternoon holiday meal becomes more vital. The table is set with the best white linen and silver. Throughout the high holy days, white holds a special meaning as it symbolizes our hope for purity and forgiveness. The wine is blessed with the kiddush; the challah similarly with the motzi. A sumptuous dinner is then served which may include sweet dishes to represent the sweet new year of forgiveness. As the sun sets that evening, the fast begins.

Some believers question whether to fast since they are already forgiven in Messiah. True, believers do not fast to obtain forgiveness, yet there are some benefits for fasting, nonetheless.

Yeshua spoke of the blessings of a fast. Although the question of salvation is already settled by faith in Yeshua, believers are still in constant need of returning to a pure walk with the father. We have sins to confess and repent of (I John 1:7–9). Fasting can sensitize our spirits to the heart of God.

Many Messianic Jews and Gentiles fast on Yom Kippur for another reason also. As it is the one day of the religious year on which Jews around the world are packed into synagogues and praying, many believers have found it to be a special day to pray for the salvation of Israel (Romans 10:1).

The evening of Yom Kippur is a wonderful time for a messianic worship service. For those who live near a messianic Jewish congregation, attending a formal Yom Kippur service can be a spiritual highlight. The music, liturgy and message all celebrate the true meaning of the day: atonement in Yeshua the Messiah!

If you are unable to attend such a group, why not plan your own service for your family and friends. You have the greatest textbook for planning such a celebration: your own Bible. Choose some songs and Scriptures that accentuate the theme of forgiveness in Yeshua. Combined with the fasting and prayer, any group has the potential for an inspiring Yom Kippur service.

By the following day, the stomach is testifying that this is a serious time of seeking God. For those who want the full Jewish experience, continue the fast, even without water, until sundown. Yom Kippur day is another time for worship services with a community of believers. The theme is the same: repentance and (for believers) rejoicing in God's plan of forgiveness.

The afternoon might be spent at home resting and further meditating on the importance of the day. Our messianic congregation has a tradition of meeting together for the final hour of daylight for a Neilah service. This has proven to be a rich time of corporate prayer and worship as we read from a messianic *siddur* (prayer book), the Scriptures, and sing songs of praise to our redeemer. As the sun sets to close Yom Kippur, we bless the wine and the challah; thus the first things we taste after the fast are sweet. Then we have a break-the-fast potluck dinner as a fitting celebration on this holy day.

Blessed be the Lord God, who has secured our salvation in Yeshua the Messiah! That is what Yom Kippur is all about for those who call on his name.

# Yom Kippur Crafts

## HEAD COVERINGS

(see directions under Shabbat)

## LAMB'S BOOK OF LIFE

**Materials:**
Large construction paper
pens

**Directions:**
Design a scroll on the paper with either end looking like it is rolled up. Write "Lamb's Book of Life" across the top and Revelation 20:12 across the bottom. Discuss the importance of being in this book, then have the child write his name in the middle.

# Yom Kippur Music

## Avinu Malkeynu

Liturgy

Sing in English: (translation)

Our Father and our King
Our Father and our King
Our Father and King
Be merciful to us
Be merciful unto us.

For we have done no deeds
Commending us unto You
For we have no deeds commending us to You
Be merciful, save us, we pray.

# Melech Ozair

*Adapted by Stuart Dauermann*
*Used by permission*

*Liturgy*

2. King, Redeemer, Savior and Shield; King, Redeemer, Savior and Shield.
Blessed art Thou, O Lord, Blessed art Thou, O Lord, Shield of Abraham.
Blessed art Thou, O Lord, Blessed art Thou, O Lord, Shield of Abraham.

3. Atah Gibbor Le'Olam va-ed; Atah Gibbor Le'Olam va-ed.
Mechayey Meytim Atah, Mechayeh Meytim Atah, Rav LeHosiah.
Mechayey Meytim Atah, Mechayeh Meytim Atah, Rav LeHosiah.

4. You are the Mighty One, forever O Lord; You are the Mighty One,
forever O Lord.
You raise the dead, sleeping in their graves, You are mighty to save.

**7**

# Sukkot

## The Feast of Tabernacles

### THE HISTORICAL BACKGROUND

*The Lord said to Moses, "Say to the Israelites: 'On the fifteenth day of the seventh month the Lord's Feast of Tabernacles begins, and it lasts for seven days. The first day is a sacred assembly; do no regular work. For seven days present offerings made to the Lord by fire, and on the eighth day hold a sacred assembly and present an offering made to the Lord by fire. It is the closing assembly; do no regular work. ("'These are the Lord's appointed feasts, which you are to proclaim as sacred assemblies, for bringing offerings made to the Lord by fire—the burnt offerings and grain offerings, sacrifices and drink offerings required for each day. These offerings are in addition to those for the Lord's Sabbaths and in addition to your gifts and whatever you have vowed and all the freewill offerings you give to the Lord.) "'So beginning with the fifteenth day of the seventh month, after you have gathered the crops of the land, celebrate the festival to the*

*Lord for seven days; the first day is a day of rest, and the eighth day also is a day of rest. On the first day you are to take choice fruit from the trees, and palm fronds, leafy branches and poplars, and rejoice before the Lord your God for seven days. Celebrate this as a festival to the Lord for seven days each year. This is to be a lasting ordinance for the generations to come; celebrate it in the seventh month. Live in booths for seven days: All native-born Israelites are to live in booths so your descendants will know that I had the Israelites live in booths when I brought them out of Egypt. I am the Lord your God.'" So Moses announced to the Israelites the appointed feasts of the Lord* (Leviticus 23:33–44).

Perhaps by now you are beginning to understand why the fall season is considered the time of the high holy days for the Jewish community. Three major holy days occur in the first nineteen days of the biblical month of Tishri (September–October). They are Rosh HaShanah, Yom Kippur and this holy day season ends with the eight days of *Sukkot* (Tabernacles).

As with the other days, the name of this holy day tells its purpose. Essentially it is two-fold, the first being related to the fall harvest. As Leviticus 23 teaches, Sukkot was to be a time of bringing in the latter harvest. It is, in other words, the Jewish "Thanksgiving." In fact, it is widely believed that the Puritan settlers, who were great students of the Hebrew Scriptures, based the first American Thanksgiving on Sukkot.

A secondary meaning of this holy day is found in the command to dwell in booths as a memorial of Israel's wilderness experience. To expand the theme of this specific historical event, we might best summarize Sukkot with the word "habitation." We know from the Torah that God dwelt with his people in their forty-year wilderness camping trip. Yet, as we camp in booths today, we should be reminded that this same faithful God watches over our lives.

With such meaningful themes, no wonder Sukkot is known as *Zman Simkhatenu* (The Time of Our Rejoicing). The fact that God provided for us and built his habitation with us is something to celebrate!

## THE TRADITIONAL JEWISH OBSERVANCE

The Torah stipulates the fifteenth of the Jewish month Tishri as the time when the Jewish people are to begin dwelling in the *sukkah* (singular for "booth") and celebrating God's provision. This holy day is so joyful, traditional Jews don't even wait for the fifteenth of Tishri to construct their sukkot. Many begin the construction five days early, immediately after the close of Yom Kippur.

The construction of the sukkah can be both challenging and fun for the whole family. The Bible gives a rather general commandment to build a sukkah; but rabbis have added great detail. Essentially, it is a temporary hut in which one is to live instead of in one's permanent house. At the very least, Jews are expected to eat some meals in the sukkah as a symbol of dwelling in it. Because it is to be a temporary structure, the sukkah appears to be flimsy. It is built outside and must have at least three walls, which may be of any material (wood, brick, tarp). If the booth is constructed next to a house, it may incorporate one or more walls of the house as its own.

The most important part of the sukkah construction is the roof. The covering for the roof (called *sechach*) can be anything that grows from the ground, such as branches, two-by-fours and bushes. Because of the prevalence of palm branches in the Middle East, it is easily understood why this foliage took a central place in the celebration of Sukkot.

To emphasize its temporary status, the roof is arranged so the stars can be seen through it on a clear night. Once the main construction of the sukkah is completed, the children contribute their part with artwork, fruit tied with string, or any other creative ideas they have. The sukkah is to be big enough to house at least one person but preferably it should be able to hold a table for meals. If the climate is mild enough, people sleep overnight in the hut.

Once the sukkah is built and the holy day has arrived, there are other customs incorporated into the celebration. As with most other Jewish holy days, the celebration starts at sundown of the first night with a festival meal. The table is set with the two traditional candlesticks and the best dining ware. An exception is sometimes made with Sukkot since many Jewish people eat their meals out in their sukkot. In such cases, a more primitive setup is as a reminder of camping in the wilderness of Sinai. In either case, the kiddush is chanted over the sweet wine; the braided challah bread is blessed and shared at the table.

Each evening of the eight-day festival, special blessings are also said over the *lulav* (palm branch) and *etrog* (citron, a fruit from Israel). These two items, along with the *hadas* (myrtle) and *arava* (willow), form what is called "The Four Species." They are wrapped together in order to be handheld for waving in every direction, symbolizing the harvest and God's omnipresence over his world. Although there seems to be a clear connection between the Four Species and the harvest theme of Sukkot, rabbis have also made some spiritual applications for these symbols.

It is taught that each of the species represents a different kind of person. The etrog, which tastes sweet and has a delightful aroma, represents a person with knowledge of the Torah and good deeds. The lulav, which comes from a date palm, has a fruit that tastes sweet, yet has no fragrance. Hence, some people have knowledge, but no good deeds. The hadas is just the opposite, having a nice fragrance yet no taste (good deeds without true knowledge). Arava, since it possesses neither taste nor smell, represents the person who lacks both knowledge and deeds. Perhaps this can serve as a reminder that faith without works is dead (James 2:17).

Traditional Jewish observance of Sukkot centers on the building of a sukkah and the blessing of the lulav with the etrog. It should also be noted that, as with the other holy days, the synagogue plays a vital role. Many synagogues build a community sukkah to enable all worshipers to experience this greatest symbol of Sukkot. Holy day services are held on the first and eighth days as stipulated by the Torah. Because Tabernacles is a time of joy, there are various processionals in which the congregants march around the aisles, waving lulavs and chanting Psalm 118: *Ana Adonai Hoshiana!* (Save us Lord!). Thus, with thanksgiving, the Jewish community seeks to remember the theme of this holy day: God dwells with his people.

## SUKKOT IN THE NEW TESTAMENT

Since Sukkot has so many rich spiritual lessons associated with it, we would expect to find some important references to it in the New Testament. Not far into the Gospel accounts of the life of Yeshua, we find the first powerful reference to Tabernacles. As the apostle John relates the special background of Messiah, he openly declares the divine nature of Yeshua. The Word not only was with God in the beginning, but this Word is the very manifestation of God himself (John 1:1)! This Word, as John calls him, was manifested to the world in a very practical and tangible way:

*The Word became a human being and lived with us, and we saw his* Sh'khinah, *The Sh'khinah of the Father's only Son, full of grace and truth* (John 1:14).

Yeshua of Nazareth is more than just a good rabbi or an intriguing philosopher. According to the Bible, he is the visible manifestation of the God of creation! Yet, did you notice the metaphor John employs to describe this incarnation of the Messiah? The Word "dwelt" among his people. The Greek word *skene* is a rich word derived from "tabernacle." In other words, as John sought to describe the Messiah's first coming to his people, the most obvious picture was the holy day Sukkot, the holy day that celebrates the dwelling of God!

There is, of course, some controversy concerning the actual date of Yeshua's birth in Bethlehem. Many believers say that since there is no definitive statement on the matter, the date can not be set with certainty. The Western Church, since the fourth century C.E., has adopted December 25 as the official day to acknowledge the incarnation of Messiah. However, most historians admit that this was more in concession to the pagans of the Roman Empire than to the Holy Scriptures.

As has often been the case, the early Church "christianized" existing pagan days and festivals to accommodate the many new converts.

December 25 is a classic case in point. It happened to be an ancient feast to celebrate the return of the sun after the winter solstice. It had nothing to do with the birth of Yeshua, but was adopted nonetheless. It seemed to later believers that there was no real evidence indicating a better date.

Unfortunately, many overlook the important evidence Sukkot provides. When the apostle John describes the birth of the Messiah, he paints it in terms of Tabernacles. The simplicity of this logic is almost astounding.

A major point of this book is to show God's plan of salvation illustrated through the holy days he revealed to Israel. Critical events regarding God's plan are consistently fulfilled on these special days. Not surprisingly, we find Messiah dying on the cross as our Passover lamb on the very day of Pesach. The pouring out of the firstfruits of God's Holy Spirit likewise takes place on the appropriate holy day of Shavuot. Would such an important event as the birth of the Messiah go unheralded by one of these biblical feasts? Of all the feasts of the Lord, Sukkot best illustrates the fact that God would dwell in the midst of his people through the presence of the Messiah. He may have literally fulfilled his promise on the very day of Tabernacles.

That the birth of Yeshua took place on Sukkot is corroborated by other evidences pointed out by Christian theologians. Some have noted that the chronological calculations in the Gospels lead us to place the birth of Messiah in the late fall. Most agree that Yeshua's earthly ministry lasted three and one-half years. Since we know he died on Passover (March/April), by backtracking we arrive much closer to Sukkot (September/October) than to December 25 (A.T. Robertson, *A Harmony of the Gospels*, p. 267).

Others have pointed out the inconsistency of shepherds watching the flocks in the fields during the dead of winter. The

*Mishna* (rabbinic commentary) states that, because of winter weather, the flocks around Bethlehem were normally brought into a protective corral called a "sheepfold" from November through February. Hence the December date seems unlikely. ("Luke," *Adam Clark's Commentary*, Vol. 5, p. 370).

A final clue surrounding the details of Messiah's birth has to do with the exceptional crowd seeking housing with the result that there was "no room in the inn" (Luke 2:7). While it is true that much of this congestion would have been related to the census taken by the Romans at that time, there seems to be more to it.

The Romans were known to take their censuses according to the prevailing custom of the occupied territories. Hence, in the case of Israel, they would opt to have people report to their home provinces at a time that would be convenient for them. There is no apparent logic to calling the census in the middle of winter. The more logical time of taxation would be after the harvest, in the fall. If this coincided with one of the major Jewish festivals, Passover, Pentecost, or Tabernacles, we would expect the entire area of Jerusalem and Bethlehem to be overrun with pilgrims.

More than likely, the nativity accounts in the Gospel took place during one of the major Jewish holy days, and not during December. The only major holy day that takes place in the fall is Sukkot. It seems that there is indeed a holy day pointing to the birth of Messiah. Messiah has "tabernacled" in the midst of his people as perfectly typified in Sukkot!

Besides the connection to the incarnation of Messiah, there are other spiritual lessons taught by this holy day. Because Sukkot was also to be a harvest festival in the late fall, it was customary to thank God for the produce of that year. It is significant to note that at this time prayers were chanted to thank God, in faith, for the upcoming winter rains essential to replenish the land.

The Talmud tells of a custom that developed in the Second Temple period which was created to illustrate this truth. At that time, during this holy day, a priest would take a water pitcher down to the Pool of *Shiloach* (Siloam), dip it in the water and carry it back to the Temple.

Crowds of people would form a huge processional behind the priest, dancing, singing and chanting the Hallel Psalms (113–118) as they entered the Temple mount. For each of the first six days of Sukkot, the processional would circle the Temple altar one time, and on the seventh day (Hoshana Rabbah) there would be seven processionals to magnify the joy.

The highlight of the ceremony came when the priest dramatically poured the water at the altar of the Temple. The response of the multitudes was so immense that the Talmud says whoever has not been in Jerusalem for this ceremony has not even experienced real joy (Sukkah 5)! Hence, it became known as *Simcha Bet Ha-sho-evah* (the Rejoicing of the House of Drawing Water).

Why all the rejoicing at this water pouring ceremony? Obviously, it had to be more than the rejoicing in the hope of future winter rains for Israel, as important as that might be. Talmudic rabbis speak of deeper truths from Isaiah 12:3 in regard to the ceremony:

> *With joy you will draw water from the wells of salvation* (Salvation in Hebrew is *yeshua*, the name of the Messiah).

More than the outpouring of temporal water in Israel, the Simcha Bet Ha-sho-evah was to prophetically illustrate the days of messianic redemption when the water of the Holy Spirit would be poured out upon all Israel (Sukkot 55). God will ultimately build his habitation with his people when the kingdom is established under Messiah's rulership. What joy this thought brought to the people's hearts!

With this historical background, we can more fully appreciate the events recorded on one particular Sukkot celebration in the New Testament.

> *Now on the last day of the festival, Hoshana Rabbah, Yeshua*
> *stood and cried out, "If anyone is thirsty, let him keep coming to*
> *me and drinking. Whoever puts his trust in me, as the Scripture*
> *says, rivers of living water will flow from his inmost being." (Now*
> *he said this about the Spirit, whom those who trusted in Him were*
> *to receive later—the Spirit had not yet been given, because*
> *Yeshua had not yet been glorified* (John 7:37–39).

Imagine the setting! Sukkot was in full swing. The joy of
the first six days was exuberant. On the great final day
(Hoshana Rabbah), the crowds were filled with expectation
for the Messiah and the Holy Spirit he would bring. At the very
time of the water drawing ceremony, Yeshua made a bold
proclamation: Do you truly want the living waters of the Holy
Spirit? Does anyone understand the true significance of this
ceremony? If anyone desires what the Bet Ha-sho-evah symbolizes, let him believe in me. I am the Messiah who will pour
out the Holy Spirit on Israel!

These were indeed radical statements; and they created
quite a stir in the Temple on that occasion.

> *On hearing his words, some people in the crowd said, "Surely this*
> *man is 'the prophet'"; others said, "This is the Messiah." But*
> *others said, "How can the Messiah come from the Galil?" (John*
> *7:40–41).*

That Yeshua of Nazareth claimed to be the promised
Messiah of the Jewish Scriptures should be uncontested.
However, the controversy surrounding the response of the
people is still manifest to this day. When properly understood, the holy day Sukkot should lead us to believe, like
many in that first-century crowd. Yeshua is who he claimed to
be: God dwelling in our midst! What a joy to experience the
living waters of his Holy Spirit as seen in the holy day Sukkot.

## THE PROPHETIC FULFILLMENT

As we have seen, there are many striking lessons to be
learned from Sukkot. God's provision, his dwelling with his
people, the joy of the holy spirit, are all themes that draw

attention to the plan written in Scripture. Yet there is still a future element remaining to be fulfilled by the Feast of Tabernacles. The apostle John tells us in his vision of final things that the reality of Sukkot will be obvious to all:

> *Then I saw a new heaven and a new earth, for the old heaven and the old earth had passed away, and there was no longer any sea. Also I saw the holy city, New Yerushalayim, coming down out of heaven from God, prepared like a bride beautifully dressed for her husband. I heard a loud voice from the throne say, "See! God's Sh'khinah is with mankind, and he will live with them. They will be his peoples, and he himself, God-with-them, will be their God"* (Revelation 21:1–3).

Sukkot was always known as the holy day that commemorates God dwelling with his people. How fitting for the Kingdom of God, when it fully comes to the redeemed earth, to be considered the ultimate fulfillment of this holy day. God himself will finally dwell with his people in all his fullness. The Sukkah of God will be among men when Messiah Yeshua dwells as the ruler of the 1000-year Messianic Kingdom!

All the Feasts of the Lord have their own particular lessons to teach. Yet, because of its latter day fulfillment, Sukkot seems to be the apex of all the other appointed times of God. The goal of God's plan is ultimately the establishment of his Kingdom on the earth. This best explains why, of all the biblical holy days, Sukkot is said to be the premier celebration of the Millennium. As the prophet Zechariah predicted:

> *Then the survivors from all the nations that have attacked Jerusalem will go up year after year to worship the King, the Lord Almighty, and to celebrate the Feast of Tabernacles. If any of the peoples of the earth do not go up to Jerusalem to worship the King, The Lord Almighty, they will have no rain* (Zechariah 14:16–17).

It is worthy to note that the judgment for not celebrating Sukkot in the Messianic Kingdom will be the withholding of rain. Since Sukkot celebrates the fall harvest, it is traditional in the Jewish community to begin the prayers for the winter rains essential for the upcoming year at this time. When

Yeshua returns to establish the long-awaited Kingdom, all people who have been redeemed by his sacrifice will gladly celebrate Sukkot in all its fullness.

What a celebration there will be as his people, both Jews and Gentiles, wave the lulav and chant, *Ana Adonai Hoshiana!* (Lord, do save us!) Amen. Come, Lord Yeshua!

## A Practical Guide for Believers in Messiah

The central element for the celebration of the Feast of Tabernacles is the booth we call the sukkah. While you may want to use the rabbinic description as a guideline (see above), you should not forget the freedom to construct this booth as you see fit. As with all biblical holy days and customs, the sukkah is a "shadow" of the greater lessons of the coming Messiah (Colossians 2:17).

Building the sukkah can be an exciting and educational family project. Whether it is a shack on the side of the house or a free-standing structure, the hut can be constructed by anyone who wants to help. The outer frame can be assembled from various materials which, in turn, can be fortified with the traditional palm branches or leaves. For this reason, Sukkot is a great time to trim up the yard as well! Children will love to add their cut out paper fruit, leaves, or Bible verses.

As previously noted, traditional Jews begin constructing the sukkah immediately after breaking the fast of Yom Kippur. Many Messianic Jews and Gentiles follow this custom by inviting people over for a "Sukkah Decorating Party," and planning for the upcoming holy day begins in earnest.

As the fifteenth day of Tishri begins, a holiday dinner is prepared. The table is set; although, being outside in the Sukkah, it will probably have a less formal atmosphere. Since this holy day is to be a reminder of the forty-year camping trip in the wilderness, the dinner will probably feel more like an outdoor picnic than a formal meal.

As with all the Jewish holy days, we start with the blessings over the fruit of the vine and the challah bread (see
appendix). The first day of the festival is also welcomed with
the Shehechiyanu blessing in order to thank God for bringing us
to this joyful celebration. Some distinctive blessings chanted
for this particular holy day are said over the sukkah as well as
the Four Species. After the blessings for the wine and challah,
the following can be recited:

Barukh atah Adonai Elohenu melekh ha-olam, asher kidshanu
b'mitzvohtav v'tzi-vanu leshev b'sukkah.

Blessed art Thou, O Lord our God, King of the universe, who has
set us apart by thy commandments and commanded us to dwell
in the Sukkah.

The above blessings are usually said only on the first night
of the holy day whenever the wine and challah are blessed.

Distinct from this is the blessing over the Four Species,
that is recounted every evening of Sukkot. (The Four Species,
"kosher from Israel," which include the lulav and the etrog,
can be ordered from Jewish gift shops or synagogues. If
unavailable, you may assemble your own symbolic version
using a palm branch, lemon, etc.) At this point, the lulav
(palm) and the etrog (citron) are picked up, the former in the
right hand, the latter in the left. Holding the two together, the
following is recited:

Barukh atah Adonai Elohenu melekh ha-olam, asher kidshanu
b'mitzvohtav v'tzi-vanu al n'tilat lulav.

Blessed art Thou, O Lord our God, King of the universe, who has
set us apart by thy commandments and commanded us to take
up the lulav.

A traditional dinner is now served, and may include some
of the produce from the harvest of this time of year. Depending upon availability in your area, local messianic congregations may have evening services to celebrate the joy found in
the message of Sukkot.

A special emphasis will be the *hakafot* (processionals), in which congregants march around the sanctuary waving the lulav and recounting the Hallel or Praise Psalms (113–118).

These major elements of the dinner in the sukkah continue for the eight days of the festival, while the synagogue services are usually convened only on the first two. To really get into the spirit of the holy day, the family might want to sleep in the sukkah under the stars, weather permitting.

As mentioned before, the seventh day of the festival has much spiritual significance for believers in Yeshua (see John 7:37 and following verses). However, as we reach the eighth day, we come to a special holiday, *Shmeni Atzeret* (literally, the Eighth Day of Assembly). As mentioned in Leviticus 23:36, this day is to be set apart as a Shabbat and a holy assembly.

Most traditional synagogues and messianic congregations have special services to remember this time. Messianic Jews and Gentiles are continually looking for the higher spiritual lessons of God's appointed times. Why would God command a special memorial on the eighth day of Sukkot? Besides being the close of the festival, this day may contain a connection to the life of Messiah. If our theory that Yeshua's birth took place on the first day of Sukkot is correct, was there anything that took place on the eighth day? Any good Jewish parent could tell you! On that day, Jewish baby boys take the sign of the Abrahamic Covenant through circumcision (Genesis 17). So, too, with Yeshua.

*On the eighth day, when it was time for his brit-milah, he was given the name Yeshua, which is what the angel had called him before his conception* (Luke 2:21).

Believers in the Messiah have good cause to remember Shmeni Atzeret. Truly Yeshua "became a servant of the Jewish people in order to show God's truthfulness by making good his promises to the Patriarchs" (Romans 15:8).

If these festivities are not enough, the Jewish community has added an additional ninth day to Sukkot called *Simchat*

*Torah* (Rejoicing in the Law). As it's name implies, this day celebrates the revelation of God as symbolized in the Torah scroll. It is a time of tremendous joy, with dancing and lively music.

A central part of the service is the reading from the last chapters of Deuteronomy and the start of the yearly cycle all over again with the first chapters of Genesis. Although this holiday was created in the Middle Ages by rabbinic Judaism, believers in Yeshua can surely affirm the idea behind it. God's Word is good. It is to be revered. It is even to be joyously celebrated! How much more so for followers of Yeshua Ha Mashiach, the Word who became flesh at this time of year!

With the close of Simchat Torah, we reach the end of the high holy day season. What wonderful truth is evident! What a complete picture of the latter-day plan of God for this world. Sometime soon the shofar will sound to announce the re-gathering of believers. This is to be followed by the solemn Day of Atonement when Yeshua will return for a second time to the earth. This, in turn, will lead all believers into that joyful celebration of the Kingdom of God at Sukkot! May we be ready to dwell in that holy habitation of our heavenly father.

# Sukkot Recipes

## FRUIT SALAD

**Ingredients:**
Ripe fruits such as melons, bananas, pineapple, peaches, nectarines and grapes.

**Directions:**
Cut melons or scoop out ball shapes. Add remaining fruits. Can serve as a side dish or dessert, adding flaked coconut or whipped cream if desired. Can serve as light meal with cottage cheese in the middle. Sprinkle with chopped walnuts if desired.

## SWEET AND SOUR CABBAGE MEATBALLS

**Ingredients:**
1 1/2 lbs. ground beef
1 large cabbage
15 or 16 ounces tomato sauce
1/4 cup brown sugar
1/4 cup lemon juice
long grain wildrice

**Directions:**
Cut a deep circle at the core of the cabbage. Place in large saucepan of boiling water for 3-5 minutes or until leaves can pull away, being careful not to overcook. Mix meat with 3/4 cup tomato sauce. Put in desired amount of rice. Roll into 12 balls. Place each in the center of cooked cabbage leaves. Place seam-side down in a large skillet. Mix remaining sauce with sugar and lemon juice. Pour over meatballs. Simmer cook, covered until done, 45 minutes to one hour. Loosen balls from the bottom of skillet occasionally while cooking.

# Sukkot Crafts

## MOBILE OR SUKKAH DECORATIONS

**Materials:**
construction paper
pens (felt makers, crayons, colored pencils)
scissors
tape
string

**Directions:**
Draw fruits or vegetables on the construction paper. Cut these out. For younger children, have cut out designs already done for them to color. If you have a sukkah, attach the decorations with tape or hang them with string. If your don't have a sukkot, hang these as a mobile using a hanger or wooden rod.

## LULAV

**Materials:**
green construction paper
scissors
tape
paper towel tubes

**Directions:**
Roll construction paper around the tube several times, with a large amount protruding from the top. Cut at the top to make long leaves.

## MINI SUKKAH

**Materials:**
empty shoe boxes
scissors
tape or glue
popsicle sticks

**Directions:**
Decorate the inside of a shoe box to create a small sukkah. Older children, who aren't in a hurry can assemble a sukkah with glue and popsicle sticks, let small children use as a "mini" doll house. Fisher Price people work best.

# 8

# ☰Hanukkah

## The Feast of Dedication

### THE HISTORICAL BACKGROUND

*Hanukkah*, or "The Feast Of Dedication," stands out among the celebrations of the Bible. This is because it does not appear among the Feasts of the Lord in Leviticus 23. Despite the fact that Hanukkah is not spoken of by Moses, we should not assume that it is therefore non-biblical. As we shall see, it is indeed mentioned in later scriptural passages.

To fully understand this holy day, go back to a tumultuous time in the history of Israel: the Hellenistic period around 167 B.C.E. As was so often the case, the Jewish people were living under the oppression of a foreign power. A few generations earlier, the Greeks had come to world power under the remarkable leadership of Alexander the Great. With the ascension of this kingdom, Alexander seemed to have unified the ancient world into one common government and culture called Hellenism.

After Alexander's untimely death, there was a political scramble among four of his generals, resulting in the division of the Hellenistic empire. The Ptolemies took control of the South, which included Egypt. The Seleucids took charge of the northern area around Syria. This left Judea caught in the middle of a tug-of-war, wondering what the outcome would be. Eventually, the Seleucid/Syrians, under the leadership of Antiochus IV, gained power and sought control of the new provinces.

Seeking to unify his holdings, Antiochus enforced a policy of assimilation into the prevailing Hellenistic culture. Irrespective of the culture and beliefs of the captured peoples, the Seleucids required submission to the Greek way of life. The Greeks thought that to be truly effective this assimilation must apply to all aspects of life, including language, the arts, and even religion. Everything was to conform to the "superior" Greek way of life and values.

Not surprisingly, this Hellenization policy did not present a major problem for many people under the Seleucids. Indeed, the Greeks were highly respected for their culture. Even many Jews in Judea had converted to the Hellenistic way and openly advocated adherence to it. However, there were a significant number of traditional Jews who were appalled at the changes in their society. Antiochus and the Seleucids continued growing more hostile towards these stubborn Jews who did not convert to Hellenism. Steps were taken to enforce their policy.

An ultimatum was given: either the Jewish community must give up its distinctive customs (Shabbat, kosher laws, circumcision, etc.) or die. To prove his point, Antiochus marched his troops into Jerusalem and desecrated the holy Temple. The altars, the utensils, even the golden *menorah* (lampstand) were all defiled or torn down. But that was just the start!

Antiochus also ordered that a pig be sacrificed on the holy altar and erected an image of the Greek god Zeus as the new point of worship in the Temple! Antiochus insisted on being called "epiphanes" (God manifest), enough to repulse any religious Jew. The Jewish community soon came up with an appropriate reflection of their feelings. Instead of calling him Antiochus Epiphanes they made a play on words, and called him "epimanes" (crazyman)!

This brutal attack on the Jewish people and their faith would not go unanswered for long. The murmurings of revolt were heard in Judea and were crystallized in a small village called Modi'in. Syrian troops entered this town to enforce their assimilation policy. The soldiers planned to erect a temporary altar to the false gods and force the populace to participate in their religious ceremony—the highlight of which was eating the flesh of the swine!

Living in this village was an old, godly priest named Mattathias and his five sons. When the Seleucid soldiers chose him to lead the pagan ceremony, Mattathias and his sons reacted with holy indignation. Enough was enough! They killed the soldiers and started a revolt against the oppressors. One of the sons, Judah, rose to leadership and was nicknamed "Maccabee" (the hammer).

Overwhelmingly outnumbered and under-supplied, the armies of the Maccabees turned to more creative devices. Relying on their knowledge of the hill country and employing guerrilla warfare, the Jewish forces met with surprising success. Spurred on by their firm conviction that the God of Israel was true and faithful, the Maccabees proved that the impossible could happen. In the Hebrew month Kislev (around December) they drove out the Syrians and recaptured the Temple in Jerusalem.

They faced the sober task of restoring the Temple to the true worship of God. The Temple compound was in shambles, desecrated by the idolatry of the Syrians. The Maccabees and their followers quickly cleansed the altars and restored the holy furnishings.

Of particular importance to them was the broken menorah, symbolizing the light of God. They restored it and attempted to light it, but there was a problem.

Jewish tradition recounts that as they searched for some specially prepared oil, they found only enough to burn for one day. The priests knew it would take at least eight days for new oil to be produced. What to do?

They decided it was better to light the menorah anyway; at least the light of God would shine forth immediately. To their amazement, the oil burned not only for one day, but for eight days until additional oil was available!

The Temple was restored and rededicated to the glory of the God of Israel and an eight-day festival was established. It is called Hanukkah (Hebrew for Dedication). Every year, starting on the twenty-fifth of Kislev, the Jewish community recalls the two-fold miracle: the miracle of the oil as well as the miraculous military victory.

Some people may question our inclusion of Hanukkah with the "biblical" holy days. It is not mentioned in the feasts of Leviticus 23. However, the *Tanakh* (Older Testament) reveals that Hanukkah is clearly predicted in later prophetic writings.

The vision given to the prophet Daniel is an amazingly, detailed description of the events surrounding Hanukkah. As he describes the coming kingdoms that would have impact on Israel, Daniel writes:

*The shaggy goat is the king of Greece, and the large horn between his eyes is the first king. The four horns that replaced the one that was broken off represent four kingdoms that will emerge from his nation but will not have the same power* (Daniel 8:21-22).

This is a graphic description of the rise of the Hellenistic empire with its strong central leader (the large horn). Alexander the Great was indeed broken by his early death. His four generals (the four horns) split the kingdom between themselves. Yet there were even more specific details given by Daniel:

*In the latter part of their reign, when rebels have become completely wicked, a stern-faced king, a master of intrigue, will arise. He will become very strong, but not by his own power. He*

*will cause astounding devastation and will succeed in whatever
he does. He will destroy mighty men and the holy people. He will
cause deceit to prosper, and he will consider himself superior.
When they feel secure, he will destroy many and take his stand
against the Prince of princes. Yet he will be destroyed, but not by
human power* (Daniel 8:23–25).

According to the word given Daniel, the focal point of this
Hellenistic kingdom would be a leader who, by a power not
his own, would persecute the Jewish people. He would magnify
himself through his brutal attacks and words, as was the case
with Antiochus who called himself Epiphanes! Yet God promised that this evil ruler would be broken without human agency.

The fanatical persecution by the Seleucids is predicted
along with the miraculous deliverance by God! The miracle of
Hanukkah is mentioned in the Hebrew Scriptures with such
detail that some liberal scholars have suggested that Daniel
was writing after the fact and not prophetically (see Walvoord's
comments on this in *Daniel*, p.16 and following pages). What
an important time of history to understand! What a great
celebration Hanukkah should be!

### THE TRADITIONAL JEWISH OBSERVANCE

Hanukkah is an enjoyable holy day with many meaningful
customs. Every year, starting on the twenty-fifth of Kislev, the
Jewish community begins its eight-day celebration. The holy
day focuses on the *hanukkiyah*, the nine-branched Hanukkah
menorah. The usual menorah, like the modern symbol of the
State of Israel, is seven-branched. Eight branches remind us
of the eight-day miracle of oil; and, the appropriate numbers
of candles are kindled each day. The ninth branch (in the
center with four branches on either side) stands out. It is used
to light the other candles and is called the *shamash* (Hebrew
for "servant"). The menorah is lit after dark, usually in connection with a festive meal.

After the blessings are said it is traditional to sing holiday
songs. Then it's time to enjoy the meal with its traditional
foods. Because of the miracle of the oil, it is customary to eat

foods cooked in oil, such as *latkes* (potato pancakes) and *sufganiot* (Israeli doughnuts). It may not be the best for our diets but it is a delicious way to remember the miracle of God at Hanukkah!

Another reminder of the miracle of this holy day is the game of *dreydels*. These wooden or plastic tops have different Hebrew letters on each of their four sides: *Nun*, *Gimel*, *Hey*, and *Shin* standing for the phrase *Nes Gadol Hayah Sham* ("A Great Miracle Happened There.") There is an interesting story behind the dreydel.

It is said that the Jewish children of Judea during the Maccabean period wanted to study Torah, but the anti-Semitic policies of the Syrians made this difficult. They came up with a creative answer: they would study the scrolls in the streets until a foreign soldier came. Then they would quickly hide the scroll, bring out the dreydels, and pretend to be engrossed in a game of tops! When the soldier left, the Torah study would begin again.

In modern celebration, dreydels are played with for fun. Each Hebrew letter has its own value for keeping score. Children are given Hanukkah *gelt* (money); which is usually foil-covered chocolate coins they use to wager with and make the game more interesting.

More recently, the custom of giving gifts has found its way into the celebration of this joyous festival. Many families give real Hanukkah gelt (money) to children, perhaps 25¢ for each year of their age. There is nothing wrong with these traditions. They are a Jewish adaptation in response to the Christmas gift-giving custom.

Often people try to establish a connection between Christmas and Hanukkah simply because they occur at the same time. However, they celebrate two entirely different events: one, the birth of the Messiah; the other, the deliverance of Israel from its oppressors. Any intermingling of the two celebrations is often man-made. Nonetheless, there are a number of compelling reasons for believers in Yeshua to celebrate Hanukkah.

## HANUKKAH IN THE NEW TESTAMENT

*Then came Hanukkah in Yerushalayim. It was winter, and Yeshua was walking around inside the Temple area, in Shlomo's Colonnade* (John 10:22–23).

Hanukkah is a beautiful holy day celebrated by Jewish people. Many are aware of the customs and history of Hanukkah. Perhaps some even know Scripture well enough to know that this holy day is prophetically mentioned in the book of Daniel. Most surprising to both the Jewish and the Christian communities is that the most clear mention of Hanukkah in the Bible is in the New Testament!

The people who normally celebrate this holy day, the Jewish people, have scant biblical references for it; yet the people who do not normally celebrate Hanukkah have the most explicit reference to it, in the New Testament!

This brings us to the first reason believers in Messiah might want to understand and celebrate this holy day. The Messiah celebrated it. Not only did Yeshua celebrate Hanukkah, but he observed it in the same Temple that had been cleansed and rededicated just a few generations earlier under the Maccabees.

Many Jewish scholars see a deeper spiritual meaning to Hanukkah. As the editors of the popular *Artscroll Mesorah Series* state:

*Then, the light is kindled to give inspiration, for the light of Messiah must burn brightly in our hearts* (Chanukah, Mesorah Publications, Brooklyn, 1981, p. 104).

This is a logical conclusion. Because Hanukkah is a celebration of deliverance, it has also become a time to express messianic hope. Just as the Maccabees were used by God to redeem Israel, perhaps the greatest redeemer, the Messiah, would also come at this time!

With this understanding, we more fully appreciate the scenes that unfolded as Yeshua celebrated the feast 2000 years ago in Jerusalem. Amidst the festivities, Yeshua was approached by some rabbis who asked a simple question: "How much longer are you going to keep us in suspense? If you are the Messiah, tell us publicly" (John 10:24). The answer to this very appropriate question is contained in Yeshua's Hanukkah message. He clearly reiterates his claim and the proofs of his Messiahship (John 10:25–39).

This shows the real connection between Hanukkah and Christmas. Hanukkah recalls a military victory for Israel, and the implications are vast. If Antiochus had succeeded in his campaign of anti-Semitism and destruction, there would have been no Jews by the time of Yeshua. The miracle of Christmas could only take place after the miracle of Hanukkah! Certainly all believers in Yeshua have important reasons to remember this Feast of Dedication. Messiah, our deliverer, has come!

## THE PROPHETIC FULFILLMENT

As with all the biblical holy days, there are spiritual lessons to be learned from Hanukkah—light, courage, and faith, to name a few. Perhaps the most vital one is seen in its name. This festival commemorates a time when the true worship of God was restored in Jerusalem. The Temple in Jerusalem no longer stands today. The heart of each true believer in Yeshua the Messiah and savior is the temple where the Spirit of God dwells. Too often believers endanger the cleanliness of this Temple by allowing idolatry into their lives. Hence the timeless exhortation from Scripture:

*Run from sexual immorality! Every other sin a person commits is outside the body, but the fornicator sins against his own body. Or don't you know that your body is a Temple for the Ruach HaKodesh (the Holy Spirit) who lives inside you, whom you received from God? The fact is, you don't belong to yourselves; for you were bought at a price. So use your bodies to glorify God* (I Corinthians 6:18–20).

May we indeed be temples for the Messiah, cleansed and dedicated for the master's use!

## A PRACTICAL GUIDE FOR BELIEVERS IN MESSIAH

In seeking a practical expression for this holy day, believers in Messiah Yeshua can incorporate many beautiful traditions. The observance is centered on the menorah and what it represents. Each evening during Hanukkah the family and friends can gather to light the menorah with the appropriate number of candles. The branches of the hanukkiyah represent the eight days of Hanukkah, plus one shamash candle used to light the others.

On the first night of Hanukkah, after sundown, the shamash candle is lit, which in turn is used to kindle one other candle in the Menorah. The second night, we light the shamash again and use it to light two candles. This continues through the eight nights of the Hanukkah. It should be noted that the appropriate numbers of candles are placed in the menorah from right to left, yet they are kindled by the shamash from left to right.

During the lighting of the shamash and the appropriate number of candles, the following blessings are chanted:

*Barukh atah Adonai Elohenu melekh ha-olam, asher kidshanu b'mitzvohtav, v'tzi-vanu l'hadleek ner, shel Hanukkah.*

*Blessed are you, O Lord our God, King of the universe, who has set us apart by your commandments and commanded us to kindle the light of Hanukkah.*

These are the traditional blessings used by Jewish people. Some believers in Messiah adapt some of the words to reflect their messianic faith. For example, "...in the name of Yeshua, the light of the world."

*Barukh atah Adonai Elohenu melekh ha-olam, she-asah nisim l'avotenu, bayamim ha-hem, bazman hazeh.*

*Blessed are you, O Lord our God, king of the universe, who has done miracles for our fathers in the days at this season.*

First Night Only Add:

*Barukh atah Adonai Elohenu melekh ha-olam, she-he-khi-yanu v'kiyamanu v'higiyanu lazman hazeh.*

*Blessed are you, O Lord our God, King of the universe, who has kept us in life, sustained us and brought us to this season.*

After lighting the candles and singing the blessings, a rousing chorus of one of the Hanukkah songs is appropriate. Then its time to sit down to a festive meal.

As you enjoy these wonderful customs, remember the important lessons associated with the Feast of Dedication.

# Hanukkah Recipes

### POTATO LATKES

**Ingredients:**
> 2 eggs
> 3 cups grated, drained potatoes
> 4 Tbls. grated onion
> 1/4 tsp. pepper
> 2 Tbls. cracker or matzah meal
> 1/2 cup oil or butter

**Directions:**

Beat the eggs and add the potatoes, onion, salt, pepper and meal. Heat half the oil or butter in a frying pan and drop the potato mixture into it by the tablespoon. Fry until browned on both sides. Keep pancakes hot until all are fried and add more oil or butter as required.

Serves 8. Serve with applesauce or sour cream.

# How to Play the Dreydel Game

The Hebrew letters N*es*, G*adol*, H*ayah*, S*ham*, mean "A miracle happened there." Those are the letters on the dreydel.

**Game Instructions**

1. *Give each person the same amount of candy or nuts.*
2. *Each player puts one piece in the pot.*
3. *The first player spins the dreydel and does what the dreydel says.*
4. *After a player gets a gimel, everyone puts one more piece into the pot.*
5. *Everyone gets a turn. When you are finished playing, you can eat your candy or nuts.*

*Gimel*—take all      *Hay*—take half      *Shin*—add 1 to pot      *Nun*—take nothing

# Hanukkah Crafts

## HANUKKIAH PICTURE

### Materials:
newspaper, poster board, glue
pictures of hanukkiahs
seeds, etc. (in bowls)

### Directions:
Spread newspaper on a table and lay the poster board on top. Show the class several real hanukkiahs (hanukkah menorahs) or pictures. Place the bowls of seeds, etc., around the table, and give each child a bottle of glue. Instruct students to spread glue, a small section at a time on portions of the hanukkiah. Have them cover the glue with seeds. Repeat for the candles and flames. Let the glue dry; shake off excess seeds onto the newspaper. Display the picture or tack it to a bulletin board.

## A SIMPLE HANUKKAH MENORAH (HANUKKIAH)

### Materials:
piece of particle board approx. 4"x10"x 1/2"
Nine 1/2" machine nuts
glue, glitter, markers

Glue eight of the nuts on the particle board, either in a straight line or in a semi-circle. Place the ninth nut slightly away from the others to serve as the "shamash." Decorate the menorah with your own design of glue and glitter or with a marking pen.

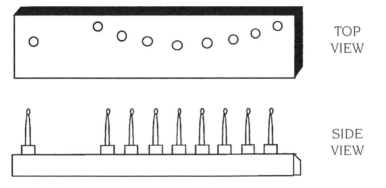

TOP VIEW

SIDE VIEW

# Maoz Tzur

Moderately                                                                 Traditional

Ma - oz    tzur    ye - shu - a - ti,        l'cha    na - ch    l' - sha -
Rock  of    A - ges,    let    our    song        Praise   Thy    sav - ing

bey - ach,        Ti - kon    bet    t' - fi - la - ti,
pow - er;        Thou,    a - midst    the    rag - ing    foes,

v'sham    to - da    n'za - be - ach.        Let    ta - chin    mat -
Wast    our    shelt - er- ing    tow - er.        Fu - rious,    they    as -

be - ach        mi - tzar        ha - m'na - be - ach,
sailed    us,        But    Thine    arm    pre - vailed    for    us,

Az    eg - mor    b' - shir    miz - mor, cha - nu - kat    ha - miz - bey - ach.
And    Thy    word        Broke    their    sword        When    our    own    strength    failed    us.

# Sevivon

Upbeat                                                                 Folk Song

Se - vi - von,    sov, sov, sov,    Ha - nu - ka        hu    hag    tov!

Ha - nu - ka    hu - hag    tov!    se - vi - von,    sov, sov, sov.

Hag  sim - ha        hu    la - am,        nes    ga - dol    ha - ya        sham!

Nes    ga - dol    ha    ya    sham!        hag    sim - ha        hu    la - am.

*Translation:*
Spin, Dreidel, spin. Hanuka is a good holiday. A great miracle happened there!

# Purim
The Feast of Lots

## THE HISTORICAL BACKGROUND

The Feast of Purim, while considered a "minor holiday" by the Jewish community, is nonetheless a time of great joy. Its important message is revealed by the name *Purim*, literally "lots." This recalls a time in Jewish history when the "lot" was cast to decide the day of destruction of the Jews. Fortunately, there is a living God who saw to it that this evil plan was never fulfilled. Purim is God's appointed time to celebrate the protection of his people from the dangers of their enemies.

To better understand this holy day, we must go to one of the more interesting times in Jewish history, the time of the first dispersion, to the land of Persia (about 450 B.C.E.). The events of Purim are recorded in the book of Esther, named after the heroine of the biblical account.

The King of Persia (modern-day Iran) was Achashveros, known as Xerxes in secular history. His was the ruling empire, having conquered the waning Babylonians. Among the multi-cultural subjects of his kingdom was the sizable Jewish remnant displaced from the land of Israel. This community had survived and flourished under the benevolence of the Persian leaders. The Jewish people felt at home in their new land and assimilated into the prevailing Persian culture. However, during the reign of Achashveros things suddenly took a turn for the worse.

The primary instigator of these problems was one of the government officials, Haman. As Haman rose to power, he insisted on the homage he felt was due him. In good pagan tradition, Haman required all the other servants to bow before him. Among the king's servants was Mordechai who had previously uncovered a plot to kill the king. Being a Jew, Mordechai was the only one who refused to bow to Haman as this would be viewed as idolatry.

Scripture says "Haman was filled with rage" at such insubordination. He desired to do away with all of the Jewish people in Persia (Esther 3) Haman devised an evil and insidious way to set the exact time of extermination (an early version of Hitler's "Final Solution") . He cast the lot (Pur in Hebrew) to set the date "to destroy, kill and annihilate all the Jews—young and old, women and little children—on a single day, the thirteenth day of the twelfth month, the month of Adar, and to plunder  their goods" (Esther 3:13).

Times could not have looked darker. As Mordechai and his people turned to fasting and prayer, a rescue plan developed. In a strange turn of events, a beautiful Jewish girl named Esther had earlier won the "Miss Shushan Contest" and been appointed as Queen of Persia. Mordechai, Esther's uncle, suddenly could see through this great "coincidence" a way the Jewish queen could help. Even though Esther had reached the pinnacle of Persian society, her uncle had some powerful words to challenge her:

*Do not think that because you are in the king's house you alone*
*of all the Jews will escape. For if you remain silent at this time,*
*relief and deliverance for the Jews will arise from another place,*
*but you and your father's family will perish. And who knows but*
*that you have come to royal position for such a time as this*
(Esther 4:13–14)?

Queen Esther had no choice but to respond to this plea.
At great risk to her own safety, she openly approached King
Achashveros with the dilemma. She requested that the king
and Haman be present at a banquet. Meanwhile, on a sleep-
less night, King Achashveros read in his court records that
Mordechai had never been recompensed for saving his life.
Through this particular "coincidence," the king decided that
he, along with his servants, should honor Mordechai for his
heroic deed. At the banquet Esther exposed the evil plot of
Haman, to which the king promptly responded by hanging
him on the very gallows Haman had built for Mordechai.

With Haman executed, the king now faced the problem of
the previous decree to destroy the Jewish people. According
to the law of the Medes and Persians, a previous law could not
be nullified; however, additional laws could be passed to
circumvent the current law. With this in mind, King
Achashveros decreed that while the Jewish community might
be open to attack, they could now defend themselves with all
the manpower they could muster. Hence, the very day appointed for destruction (13 Adar) became a day of deliverance
and great joy for the Jewish community as they successfully
repelled the attacks of their enemies. Such is the history of the
Feast of Purim, as is recorded near the end of the scroll of Esther:

*Mordechai recorded these events, and he sent letters to all the Jews*
*throughout the provinces of King Xerxes, near and far, to have*
*them celebrate annually the fourteenth and fifteenth days of the*
*month of Adar as the time when the Jews got relief from their*
*enemies, and as the month when their sorrow was turned into joy*
*and their mourning into a day of celebration. He wrote them to*
*observe the days as days of feasting and joy and giving presents*
*of food to one another and gifts to the poor.... Therefore these days*
*were called Purim, from the word Pur (lot) (Esther 9:20–22,26).*

The God of Israel proven himself faithful to his promises to watch over Israel once again (see Genesis 12:3), and that is something to celebrate!

## THE TRADITIONAL JEWISH OBSERVANCE

Since the time of Esther and Mordechai, the holy day of Purim has held a distinct place on the Jewish calendar. The dates of the festival are clearly stated in the book of Esther, although there has been some adaptation over the years. The date chosen by Haman for the destruction of the Jews was the thirteenth of the biblical month of Adar. To remember the somberness of that time, the traditional Jewish community begins a fast that day every year, from sundown to sundown. This also recalls the time when Mordechai and Esther began a three-day fast as they sought God's guidance (Esther 4:16). Because of the mighty deliverance on that day, the joyful celebration of Purim begins at sunset on 14 Adar and continues through 15 Adar. The second day is often called *Shushan Purim* because the Jews celebrated for an extra day in Persia (Esther 9:18).

As the book of Esther indicates, Purim is to be a time of great rejoicing by "feasting and rejoicing and sending portions of food to one another and gifts to the poor" (Esther 9:22). Each of these components is integrated into the modern celebration of Purim.

Feasting is remembered through a festive meal (called *Seudah*) with family and friends, or at the synagogue. This takes place in the afternoon of the first day of Purim. The spirit of feasting continues throughout the entire period.

As with other Jewish holy days, there is traditional food that has symbolic significance. In the case of Purim, it is the delicious *hamantashen* cookies. These are triangular and stuffed with jam or some other sweet filling. Hamantashen, a German/Yiddish word, can mean "Haman's pockets" or, as the Hebrew (*Ozney Haman*) says, "Haman's ears." These interesting treats remind people of the victory over this awful antagonist.

The "rejoicing" aspect of Purim is seen in other elements. Along with the joyous feast of this holy day, the central focus in the synagogue service is joy. Because the history of Purim is found in story form, the scroll of Esther (Megillat Esther) is chanted in Hebrew as a dramatic way of recounting the events. This takes place on the first evening of Purim, and may be accompanied by a dramatic reenactment called a Purim Shpiel. Here the rejoicing becomes full-force. As the scroll is read, the villain, Haman, is vigorously booed at every mention of his name. To blot out his name, noisemakers called groggers are used, sometimes at a deafening volume! By contrast, every mention of the hero, Mordechai, is followed by a thunderous cheer.

Purim is one of the few synagogue holy days when normal decorum and seriousness are waived in order to enter into unrestrained joy. Through the reading of the Megillah, the shpiel and the party atmosphere, the true joy of deliverance is felt. Rabbinic tradition goes so far as to say that one should partake of the joy and drink until one does not even know the difference between Haman and Mordechai (Megillot 7b)! This attitude is extreme, but it does illustrate the great joy associated with the Feast of Purim.

As written in the Scriptures, Purim is not only to be a celebration for the redeemed Jews, but also a time to send gifts to the poor of the community (Esther 9:22). The Hebrew term mishloach manot is often translated shlach manos in Yiddish, meaning "sent portions." These shlach manos boxes may include food, sweets and hamantashen. It is one of the ways Jewish people are reminded to help those who are less fortunate.

Some rabbis note a messianic aspect to this holy day. Being a day of deliverance and rest from one's problems, Purim was naturally related to the greater day of rest in the days of Messiah. As one commentary relates:

> The Patriarch Jacob had longed to institute that every day of the week be like the Sabbath of messianic times—totally saturated with the holiness of that Sabbath—but he was unsuccessful, for

it was premature. He was successful, however, in that his descendants would be able to experience some taste of this messianic Sabbath even during the week, at such times as Chanukah and Purim (Sfas Emes, as quoted in the Artscroll Series book on Chanukah, p. 107).

Indeed, Purim is a grand reminder of God's plan for his world and how that plan will be implemented through the coming of Messiah!

## THE PROPHETIC FULFILLMENT

The holy day of Purim is not directly mentioned in the New Covenant, but the lessons of this feast permeate it. The main lesson is found in the faithfulness of God towards his covenant people. In Genesis 12:3 we find that part of the promise to Abraham is divine protection: "I will bless those who bless you, and whoever curses you I will curse; and all peoples on earth will be blessed through you." The simple but profound lesson of Purim is that God will be faithful to his promises. Anytime his people are threatened with destruction, God will intervene because his character is at stake. As Rabbi Saul of Tarsus put it, "for God's free gifts and his calling are irrevocable" (Romans 11:29). Perhaps the best one-word summary of all this is found in the word "protection."

Yet the message of Purim is not to be limited to the ancient history of Israel. Every believer in Yeshua has reason to celebrate. God's consistent protection of the Jewish people should give all believers a sense of hope and security. God is a covenant-keeping God who is faithful to every generation.

A secondary yet important lesson of this holy day is the responsibility of man to accomplish God's will. Esther is the only book of the Bible with no clear reference to God; yet he can be seen working out his perfect plan behind the scenes. Also emphasized is that people have a responsibility to act if the will of God is to be carried out. When the evil plot of Haman became known to the Jewish community of Persia, there was a call to prayer and fasting. Ultimately, there was also a call to action as seen in the exhortation from Mordechai to Queen Esther:

*For if you remain silent at this time, relief and deliverance will arise for the Jews from another place, but you and your father's family will perish. And who knows but that you have come to royal position for such a time as this* (Esther 4:14)?

Jewish people today are facing another imminent danger. There may not be a threat of physical destruction as in the days of Haman, but there is an even more dangerous threat of spiritual catastrophe for many who are far from the God of their fathers and the appointed Messiah. Undoubtedly, God is drawing many Jewish people to Yeshua in these latter days. But the laborers are too few. Purim should be a reminder to all believers that God desires to use people who are available to serve in the kingdom. Who knows whether you have not been placed where you are for such a time as this? May we all be faithful ambassadors of Messiah bringing the message of spiritual redemption to those around us.

## A PRACTICAL GUIDE FOR BELIEVERS IN MESSIAH

As you can see by now, Purim is perhaps the most expressive feast in the biblical calendar. The normal synagogue decorum is temporarily set aside for the noisy joy of celebration. As with most of the other holy days, many of the Jewish customs can be incorporated into a messianic expression. For example, while not commanded in Scripture, the Fast of Esther on the thirteenth of Adar certainly fits the spirit of prayer and fasting also taught in the New Covenant. Believers might choose this day to intercede for the protection and salvation of Israel (see Romans 10:1).

At the close of the Fast, the first day of Purim begins with the synagogue service and the reading of the Megillah. Because it is considered a minor holy day, the usual meal with candles is not required. However, preparation for the synagogue service compensates for what is passed over regarding the meal.

Since there will be a traditional reading of the book of Esther, all participants are encouraged to dress in costume (biblical or otherwise) to facilitate the role-playing. There are usually many little Esthers and Mordechais at the service—even a few bold Hamans! It is also a good time to let inhibitions go: hence there may be people dressed as anyone from the President of the United States to Mickey Mouse! Think of Purim as a sanctified costume party with an important message.

Along with the fun of dressing in costume, all participants are encouraged to bring noisemakers. These may be official groggers that can be bought in a Jewish gift shop, or home-made inventions (pots with a spoon, percussion instruments, etc.) When Haman's name is mentioned these noisemakers are activated. If you are creative, you may want to write an original Purim shpiel that can be acted out to describe the story of Esther. Believers in Messiah can enjoy the meaning of these customs, rejoicing in God's justice and protection.

The day of Purim is set aside for the blessing of the shlach manos gift boxes. You may want to have a hamantashen baking party to prepare these tasty cookies. What an encouragement it would be for a friend or acquaintance to receive a love gift of goodies, especially in the name of Yeshua. Indeed, there is more happiness in giving than in receiving (Acts 20:35).

Most messianic congregations have Purim services. If you don't happen to live within reach of one, why not invite some friends over for your own Purim celebration? It can be a wonderful time of learning and rejoicing in the faithfulness of the God of Israel.

It is the same God who desires to bless our personal lives today. Purim is a time of great joy for believers in Yeshua HaMashiach!

# Purim Recipes

### HAMANTASHEN

•Note: Dough should be made and refrigerated several hours or overnight before using.

**Ingredients:**
  1 cup butter or margarine
  1 cup sugar
  2 egg yolks
  1/2 teaspoon salt
  3 cups flour
  1 teaspoon baking powder
  1/3 cup milk
  Flour for rolling
  Fillings

**Directions:**
    Cream butter, sugar yolks and vanilla. Mix in the dry ingredients and milk. Divide recipe into two and store in wax paper in refrigerator. After dough is chilled, roll on floured board until 1/8 inch think. Cut into circles using a cup as a cutter. Place on cookie sheet. Put a little filling in each center. Fold 3 sides up to form a triangle. Bake at 350° for 8–10 minutes.

**Fillings:**
    Can use chopped pie fillings, jams, prpared can fillings such as prune, apricot or poppyseed. Two fillings that we make are as follows.

**Date Filling Ingredients:**
  1 lb. cut up dates
  1/4 cup sugar
  1 1/2 cups water.

**Directions:**
    Place ingredients in a saucepan and cook over low heat for 10 minutes, stirring constantly until mixture thickens. Cool before using. This recipe will fill at least 3 batches of hamentashen dough.
    (*See next page for more filling recipes.*)

**Apricot-Cheese Filling Ingredients:**
8 oz. cream cheese, softened
4 oz. finely chopped, dried apricots
sugar to taste

**Directions:**
Cream the softened cream cheese then add the sugar and apricots.

## "Daniel" Lentil Soup

**Ingredients:**
1 onion
1 lb. chicken parts, without skin
2 tablespoons oil
2 carrots
2 celery stalks
4 cups water
16 oz. can tomato juice
1/2 lb. lentils
1/2 teaspoon each garlic, pepper and parsley

**Directions:**
Chop the onion and put in a pot with chicken and oil. Saute for 5 minutes, stirring occasionally. Peel the carrots. Cut carrots and celery into 1/2 inch pieces and add to the pot.

Add water, juice, lentils and spices. Bring to a boil, lower heat and simmer covered for 1 1/2 hours until lentils are soft. Remove chicken and bones. Chop the chicken and return to the soup.

# Purim Crafts

### GROGGERS (NOISE MAKER)

**Materials:**
small paper plates or toilet paper tubes
pens (felt makers, crayons, colored pencils)
stapler or masking tape
dry beans or popcorn.

**Directions:**
For plate noise makers, have the children decorate the backs of the plates. Put some beans or popcorn between the plates. Staple sides, making sure that none of the beans/ popcorn can fall out. You may seal the edges of the plates with masking tape instead of staples.

For tube noise maker, decorate the tube as it is. Cover one end of tube with paper, put in some beans or popcorn. Finish by covering the other end the same way as the first end.

### SHOPPING BAG COSTUMES

**Materials:**
large paper grocery bags
scissors
pens (felt markers, crayons, colored pencils)
paint—optional

**Directions:**
Hats—Roll the bag up, leaving a crown. Paint the crown and leave to dry.
Jackets—Cut up the middle on a wide side. Make a head hole at the top of the middle. Cut out two arm holes on each side, then decorate.

# Purim Music
## Hag Purim

*Upbeat*                                                                                      *Folk Song*

Hag  Pu - rim,    hag  Pu - rim,    hag  ga - dol  hu
Pu - rim's  here,  Pu - rim's  here,  Joy - est  time  in

la - yehu - dim,   Ma - se - hot,   ra - sha - nim,
all  the  year.    Mask  your  eyes,  in  dis - guise,

shi - rim  veri - ku - dim.    Ha - va  nar - i - sha,
Sing  out  loud  and  cheer!    Turn  the  grog - gers

rash,  rash,  rash,    Ha - va  nar - i - sha,  rash,  rash,  rash,
rash,  rash,  rash.    Turn  the  grog-gers,  rash,  rash,  rash.

Ha - va  nar - i - sha,  rash,  rash,  rash,  ba - ra - sha - nim.
Turn  the  grog-gers,  rash,  rash,  rash.  Now  that  Pu - rim's  here.

# Conclusion

## The Joy of the Holy Days

What an amazing journey it is to travel through the biblical feasts! With this overview we have seen some of the rich heritage believers in Yeshua possess. The holy days are not only God's reminders of his past faithfulness, but also of his future plans for the world at the return of Yeshua the Messiah.

My prayer is that this book will be a valuable tool for understanding God better. Likewise, it is my hope that all believers can celebrate their faith as these days are incorporated into their spiritual lives.

Most importantly, I trust that as the biblical holy days are understood and experienced they will give a renewed sense of joy. Each feast and festival, each custom and tradition draws our attention to the present redemption in Messiah and the coming Kingdom of God. No wonder the Torah says to "rejoice in your feasts!"

May that spiritual joy be yours in a fresh way as you celebrate the full meaning of God's appointed times.

# BIBLIOGRAPHY

Berkowitz, Richard and Michelle Berkowitz. *Shabbat—Celebrating The Sabbath The Messianic Jewish Way*. Baltimore: Lederer Messianic Publications, 1991.

Booker, Richard. *Jesus In The Feasts Of Israel*. South Plainfield: Bridge Publishing, 1987.

Buksbazen, Victor. *The Gospel In The Feasts Of Israel*. Fort Washington: Christian Literature Crusade, 1978.

Cohen, A. *The Five Megilloth*. New York: Soncino Press, 1983.

Cohn, Haim. *The Trial And Death Of Jesus*. New York: Ktav Publishing House, 1977.

Donin, Rabbi Hayim Halevy. *To Be A Jew*. New York: Basic Books, 1972.

Edersheim, Alfred. *The Life And Times Of Jesus The Messiah*. Grand Rapids: Eerdmans Publishing, 1984.

_____. *The Temple*. Grand Rapids: Eerdmans Publishing, 1978.

*Encyclopedia Judaica*. Jerusalem: Keter Publishing House, 1972.

Fischer, John, and David Bronstein. *Siddur For Messianic Jews*. Palm Harbor, FL: Menorah Ministries, 1988.

Fruchtenbaum, Arnold. *Hebrew Christianity: Its Theology, History And Philosophy*. San Antonio: Ariel Press, 1983.

Fuchs, Daniel. *Israel's Holy Days In Type And Prophecy*. Neptune, N.J.: Loizeaux Brothers, 1988.

Glaser, Mitch and Zhava Glaser. *The Fall Feasts Of Israel*. Chicago: Moody Press, 1987.

Hilton, Rabbi Michael and Father Gordian Marshall. *The Gospels and Rabbinic Judaism*. Hoboken: Ktav Publishing House, 1988.

Hoehner, Harold. *Chronological Aspects Of The Life Of Christ*. Grand Rapids: Zondervan, 1977.

Juster, Daniel. *Jewish Roots*. Pacific Palisades: Davar, 1986.

Kasdan, Sara. *Love And Knishes*. New York: Vanguard Press, 1969.

Klausner, Joseph. *Jesus Of Nazareth*. New York: Menorah Publishing Company, 1979.

Klein, Isaac. A Guide To Jewish Religious Practice. New York: The Jewish Theological Seminary Of America, 1979.

Lachs, Samuel Tobias. A Rabbinic Commentary On The New Testament. Hoboken: Ktav Publishing House, 1987.

Levitt, Zola. The Seven Feasts Of Israel. Dallas: Zola Levitt Ministries, 1979.

McQuaid, Elwood. The Outpouring. Bellmawr, N.J.: Friends of Israel Gospel Ministry, 1990.

Patai, Raphael. The Messiah Texts. New York: Avon Books, 1979.

Renberg, Dalia Hardof. The Complete Family Guide To Jewish Holidays. New York: Adama Books, 1985.

Robertson, A.T. A Harmony Of The Gospels. New York: Harper and Row, 1922.

Rosen, Moishe and Ceil Rosen. Christ In The Passover. Chicago: Moody Press, 1978.

Rubin, Barry and Steffi. The Messianic Passover Haggadah. Baltimore: Messianic Jewish Publishers, 1989.

Rubin, Barry and Steffi. The Messianic Passover Seder Preparation Guide. Baltimore: Messianic Jewish Publishers, 1989.

Scherman, Rabbis Nosson and Meir Zlotowitz. Chanukah—Its History, Observance And Significance. Brooklyn: Mesorah Publications, 1989.

Siegel, Richard and Michael and Sharon Strassfeld. The First Jewish Catalog. Philadelphia: The Jewish Publication Society.

Silverman, Rabbi Morris. Sabbath And Festival Prayer Book. U S A : United Synagogue Of America, 1979.

Thomas, Robert and Stanley Gundry. A Harmony Of The Gospels. Chicago: Moody Press, 1979.

Walvoord, John. Daniel—The Key To Prophetic Revelation. Chicago: Moody Press, 1977.

Wolfson, Ron. The Art Of Jewish Living—The Passover Seder. New York: The Federation Of Jewish Men's Clubs, 1988.

Zimmerman, Martha. Celebrate The Feasts. Minneapolis: Bethany House Publishers, 1981.

# About the Author

Barney Kasdan is the leader of Kehilat Ariel of San Diego California, one of the largest and most successful congregations in the world.

He received a B.A. from Biola University and a Master of Divinity degree from Talbot Theological Seminary in Southern California. He also did a year of post-graduate study at the University of Judaism.

He and his wife Liz reside in San Diego with their children.